Magic Slippers

STORIES FROM THE BALLET

Magic Slippers

BY GILDA BERGER
ILLUSTRATED BY VERA ROSENBERRY

Hodder & Stoughton
LONDON SYDNEY AUCKLAND

British Library Cataloguing in Publication Data

Berger, Gilda
Magic slippers.
1. Ballet
I. Title   II. Rosenberry, Vera
792.8

ISBN 0-340-54857-6

Text copyright © Gilda Berger 1990
Illustrations copyright © Vera Rosenberry 1990

First published 1990 by Doubleday, New York, USA
First published in Great Britain 1991
Second impression 1993

Published by Hodder and Stoughton Children's Books,
a division of Hodder and Stoughton Ltd,
Mill Road, Dunton Green, Sevenoaks, Kent TN13 2YA

Printed in Hong Kong

Contents

Introduction

Ballet is an art form that uses dancing, music, costumes, and scenery to tell a story or create an atmosphere. The story, often an action-packed adventure, is about magic and mystery, fairies and witches, princes and princesses, ogres and monsters, puppets and dolls, exotic lands and enchanted kingdoms. While the story a ballet tells stays mostly the same from production to production, different companies can and do vary details and overall approach.

Of the hundreds and hundreds of ballets that have been made, a small handful are performed year after year by professional and amateur ballet companies, and by schools of ballet all around the world. These are generally considered the 'great' classical ballets. By and large, the stories on which these ballets are based are also well-loved. People, young and old, enjoy these fascinating tales over and over again.

Even though the history of ballet goes back about four centuries, ballet, as we know it, came of age about 150 years ago. This was about the time ballerinas first learned to dance on point. Dancers discovered the *plié*, the bend at the knee that makes high jumps possible. Now able to rise to their toes and jump high (without the use of wires and other machinery), ballerinas could become out-of-this-world creatures of fantasy.

Around this same period, the 1830s and 1840s, the invention of gas lighting enabled designers to produce special effects on the stage. Gas lighting could create eerie mistiness, half-darkness, and blackness, which were not possible with candles. Generally speaking, the dances which were made during this time are called Romantic ballets.

La Sylphide opened in Paris in 1832, and was an immediate and lasting success. The story concerns a sylphide, an imaginary winged creature who lives in the air. The Sylphide comes into the life of a young Scotsman, James, who is about to be married. She lures James away to her enchanted forest. Once there, James finds he cannot catch the Sylphide. Madge, a witch, suggests that he wrap a magic scarf around the creature. Unable to foresee the result of his action, James follows the witch's advice. But when he does, all hope for happiness is lost.

The ballet *Giselle* dates from 1841. It has been nicknamed the *Hamlet* of ballet because it is charged with emotion and timeless. The whole story can be briefly summarised: a young peasant girl, Giselle, is betrayed by her fiancé, Albrecht. As a result, she loses her sanity and dies. The girl becomes a spirit but finds a way to show Albrecht that she loves and forgives him.

Russian ballets of the 1890s set a standard for ballet that has never been surpassed. Ballets from mid-nineteenth-century to late-nineteenth-century Russia are part of the Classical or 'golden age' of ballet. The three most famous classical ballets, and among the most popular ballets of all time, are *The Sleeping Beauty* (1890), *The Nutcracker* (1892), and *Swan Lake* (1895).

A well-known fairy tale by Charles Perrault is the basis for the story of *The Sleeping Beauty*. At her christening, the baby Princess Aurora is condemned by an evil fairy to prick her finger and die. The good Lilac Fairy saves her with a gift that will cause her to sleep, not die, until awakened by the kiss of a prince.

The story of *The Nutcracker* comes from a tale by E. T. A. Hoffmann, a German storyteller who had a special interest in black magic and witchcraft. Set on Christmas Eve early in the nineteenth century, the adventure focuses on a young girl, Marie (called Clara in some productions), who receives a Nutcracker doll from her godfather, Drosselmeyer. The Nutcracker later changes into a handsome young prince, who takes Marie to an enchanted land of magical dreams.

Swan Lake concerns Prince Siegfried, who falls in love with Odette, the Swan Queen, a beautiful young woman under the spell of an evil sorcerer, Von Rotbart. The Swan Queen heads a flock of swan maidens who, like herself, are condemned to be swans from dawn to midnight and women from midnight to dawn. The Prince swears his eternal love to the Swan Queen and plans to marry her. But the wicked Von Rotbart contrives a way to keep the lovers apart.

Comic ballets, lighthearted and fun works, are about ordinary people, not royalty or supernatural heroes. *Coppélia* (1870), the most famous comic ballet of all time, was composed between the height of Romanticism (marked by *Giselle*) and the Russian school of Classicism (*Swan Lake*, *The Nutcracker*, and *The Sleeping Beauty*).

The story of *Coppélia*, also taken from a tale by E. T. A. Hoffman, involves a spirited young girl named Swanilda, who is in love with a youth named Franz. Swanilda believes that Franz loves Coppélia, who is, in reality, a completely lifeless doll made by Dr Coppélius. But through some comical twists and turns, Franz comes to realise that love is best when it can be returned.

A few ballets of the twentieth century follow nineteenth-century concepts. Love is almost always the central theme. These ballets usually have spectacular sets, large casts, and magical effects. The two most popular 'traditional' twentieth-century ballets are *Romeo and Juliet* (1938) and *Cinderella* (1945).

Romeo and Juliet is based on the famous play of the same name by William Shakespeare. The plot revolves around the long-standing rivalry between two families, the Montagues and the Capulets. Romeo, a Montague, falls in love with Juliet, a Capulet, and they are secretly married. Immediately after the wedding ceremony, Romeo slays

Tybalt, a Capulet, and is banished. Juliet hatches a plan to take a potion that will make her seem dead so that she can escape and be with Romeo. But the plan fails and the outcome is both shocking and sad.

The familiar story of Cinderella is based on *Cendrillon*, a fairy tale by Charles Perrault. Poor Cinderella is left at home while her cruel stepsisters go to the Prince's ball. A beggar-woman appears, and is magically transformed into Cinderella's fairy godmother. She produces an outfit for Cinderella to wear to the ball, including a pair of glass slippers. She also warns Cinderella to be home by midnight when the spell will be broken. While dancing with the handsome Prince, Cinderella hears the clock strike twelve and flees, dropping one slipper. The Prince finds it and searches the kingdom for the girl who fits the tiny slipper.

The twentieth century has also developed a kind of ballet that leans toward the experimental or modern. The best known of these dances are *Firebird* (1910) and *Petrouchka* (1911).

The theme of *Firebird* comes from a Russian legend, and like other such legends concerns the victory of a good man over one who is evil and powerful. In this story, Prince Ivan does a favour for the magical Firebird, who gives him a feather to protect him against danger. When the Prince wanders into the strange garden of the cruel Kastchei, he falls in love with a beautiful princess who is being held prisoner there. Prince Ivan uses the special powers of the Firebird's feather to fight the wicked ogre and try to free the Princess.

Set at the Shrovetide Fair in the Russian city of St Petersburg early in the spring of 1830, *Petrouchka* is a love story involving three puppets. The hero, Petrouchka, is the clown who laughs through his tears. He is in love with the very beautiful Ballerina. But the Ballerina loves the Moor, a giant of a man, not very clever or kind; but strong – and also in love with the Ballerina. At the end, no one is really sure if these characters are just puppets of cloth and sawdust or something more.

Now turn the page – and meet some of the incredible characters who live in the magical world of ballet.

La Sylphide

Late on the morning of his wedding day, James was dozing in a chair by the fire. Already dressed for the ceremony in kilt and cap with feather, the young, good-looking Scotsman moved restlessly, as though dreaming.

Kneeling at his feet, with an adoring look in her eyes, was the very creature he had been dreaming about. She was a slender, graceful, fairylike being called a sylphide – a mortal creature without a soul, who lived in the air rather than on earth. Humans rarely (if ever) see a sylphide. But in the year 1830, in that remote farmhouse in Scotland, a sylphide did appear.

After a while, the Sylphide arose. Her two light, thin wings extended from the lovely curve of her shoulders. She wore a tight-bodiced, filmy, bell-shaped dress and a small crown that sparkled on her head. Playfully she began to dart and leap around James's large, high-backed chair. Then, very gently, she leaned over and kissed the handsome lad on his forehead.

James stirred and jumped awake. The dainty Sylphide stood in front of him.

'You are the prettiest woman I have ever seen,' he whispered respectfully.

The fragile creature fluttered her eyelashes with childish delight and started to dance again. Lovingly, she circled his chair and teased him with flirtatious smiles and coquettish glances.

James stood up and moved toward the enchanting Sylphide. 'Let me hold your hand,' he beseeched.

But she danced away from him to the fireplace. A moment later, she vanished in the smoke curling up from the embers.

'I think I've fallen in love with that delightful creature,' James said to himself, in true wonderment. 'But is she real? Or is she part of a dream?'

James looked deep into the fireplace for another glimpse of the winged beauty. So occupied was he, that he barely noticed Effie, his bride-to-be, and Gurn, his best friend, who had just entered the room.

After an awkward moment, Gurn said to Effie, 'Well, if your fiancé won't give you a good-morning kiss, then I will!' The blushing girl smiled as Gurn kissed her on the cheek.

Gurn was so much in love with Effie himself that he was moved to say, 'Even now, I would give everything for you to be my bride.'

The girl laughed lightly and took Gurn's hand. 'You are very sweet,' she said, 'and I do care for you a great deal. But I love James and am marrying him today.'

Gurn shook his head sorrowfully. 'But you could still change your mind and marry me.'

'Away with you,' James called out, having overheard Gurn's last comment. 'Today is my wedding day,' he said, 'and I'm going to kiss my bride.'

'I have long awaited this day,' James continued, holding both of Effie's hands and looking into her lovely eyes. Forgetting the Sylphide for a moment, he went on to say, 'I love only you and I love you very much.'

By then, members of the wedding party started to arrive. Effie's cheerful bridesmaids, dressed in bright plaids, bustled in bearing gifts of flowers, cloth, and jewelry. The bride, delighted with her presents, tried on the jewelry and wrapped the cloth around her shoulders.

Unknown to her, James had wandered back to the fire. His mind was once again filled with thoughts of the Sylphide.

Suddenly, in the midst of everything, the old, grizzle-haired fortune-teller, Madge, entered the house. Bent over her crooked walking stick, she hobbled into the room and huddled before the fire trying to warm herself. She was a frightful sight. Her ragged clothes were dirty. Uncombed hair hung around her deathly pale face in long, straggly strands.

'Fortunes, fortunes,' she cackled. 'Does anyone want a fortune told?'

The girls were happy to see Madge and ran over to her. But James frowned. He was disgusted by the hag's unkempt and slovenly appearance. And he was annoyed at the disturbance she caused. 'Out! Get out!' he growled, rushing towards her.

Gurn held back the irate James and bid Madge welcome. When the bridegroom finally broke free of Gurn's grip, he stalked away and stared moodily into the fire.

Effie was the first to ask Madge to tell her fortune. 'Will I be happy in marriage?' the young girl asked.

'Yes, my dear,' the old woman responded. 'You will.'

'Well, then,' Effie went on, 'does James love me?'

Old Madge shook her head. 'No. He does not.' At that, the fortune-teller broke into a loud, scary laugh as though she enjoyed bringing Effie such bad news.

Having overheard the conversation, James grew very angry. He picked up the broom by the fireplace and began chasing Madge.

'Out, out, you witch!' he shouted. 'Your fortune-telling is a pack of lies. We don't want to hear them.'

Only one step ahead of James's broom, the hag scurried out of the room as fast as her short legs would carry her.

Once she was gone, Effie turned to James, and in a worried tone asked, 'Do you really love me?'

'Of course I do,' he replied. 'Don't listen to the ravings of a crazy old lady.'

One by one, everybody left to get dressed for the wedding. Still puzzled and disturbed by the Sylphide, James was left alone again. Suddenly he became aware of a cold draft in the room. Turning toward the window, he saw the Sylphide looking very sad and troubled.

'What is wrong?' he asked. 'Why are you so downcast?'

'I've loved you from afar for many years,' the Sylphide confessed. 'I have always hoped that someday we might be wed. Now you are marrying Effie. There is no more hope for me.'

The Sylphide started to weep. 'If I cannot be your bride', she sobbed, 'I do not wish to live.'

James was touched by the Sylphide's words. Going down on his knees before her, he whispered, 'Since we met, my love for you has been growing and growing. I have tried to forget you. But I cannot. I love you as much as you love me.'

Instantly, the Sylphide's mood changed. She became very sprightly and high-spirited. Joyously, she began to clap her hands and gaily skip around the room. Pleased that he could make her so happy, James caught the Sylphide in a warm embrace and gave her a long, lingering kiss.

At that very moment, Gurn entered the room and saw them locked in each other's arms. Neither James nor the Sylphide noticed him.

Here's my chance, Gurn thought. I'll call Effie. If she sees James with another woman, she will leave him and marry me.

Gurn dashed to get Effie, who came at once. James heard them approaching. 'Quick,' he whispered to the Sylphide, 'you must hide.'

'Where? Where?' The Sylphide looked frantically around the room. 'Ah, here. I'll nestle in your chair. Just cover me with the shawl.'

No sooner was the Sylphide concealed, than Effie, in her bridal gown, rushed into the room with Gurn. 'I saw you kissing another woman,' Gurn accused James. 'Where is she?'

James laughed. 'I've been alone all this while. There is no one here. Look for yourself if you don't believe me.'

Gurn looked around. 'I don't see anyone,' he said hesitatingly. But then his eyes fell on the shawl covering the chair. 'Ah-hah, what's this?'

James was very frightened. 'Wait – ' he started to say. But Gurn grabbed the shawl and whisked it away. Much to James's surprise, the chair was empty. The Sylphide had disappeared!

'Your jealousy must be making you see things,' Effie said to Gurn angrily.

'But – but – I was sure I saw them together,' Gurn mumbled, as he continued to search the room.

It was now time for the wedding to begin. The band tuned up for a high-spirited Scottish reel. Each couple took its position for the dance. But when Effie looked for James, she found him gazing out of the window.

'Don't you want to dance with me?' Effie asked coyly.

'Uh – uh . . . ' James stuttered, his mind obviously very far away. 'Of course I do,' he finally replied. And taking her hand, he led his bride to the head of the line for the dance.

Soon everyone was joyfully performing the vigorous Scottish reel. James, especially, threw himself into the gay, rollicking dance with wild abandon.

All at once, the Sylphide appeared. She flitted between the dancing guests, taking care not to touch anyone. James alone noticed her.

As she darted to and fro, James kept turning to watch her. The guests wondered at his agitation and the strange steps he was doing. But Effie, in love and very happy on her wedding day, noticed nothing.

When the dance ended, the wedding ceremony got under way. The crowd gathered around the couple. James looked into Effie's eyes and started to slip the ring on her finger. At that instant, the Sylphide shot out from nowhere and snatched the ring from his hand. She paused a moment, then floated noiselessly through the open window and toward the forest.

Almost as fast, James wheeled away from his waiting bride and raced after his dream-love.

Left behind, Effie collapsed and fell to the floor. Her parents and bridesmaids rushed to comfort her.

Gurn stepped forward. 'James is running away with another woman,' he informed the shocked guests. 'Let's give chase and bring back the blackguard!'

Gurn beckoned his friends to follow. And off they dashed into the dark woods in search of the missing bridegroom.

In the midst of the ominous forest lived the fortune-teller Madge and her band of evil witches. Hideous and hunchbacked, they were dressed in filthy, tattered garments. Their hissing, grating speech was peppered with outbreaks of high-pitched, cackling laughter.

On this evening, Madge and the other witches were doing a magic ritual dance around a smoky fire. The orange flames shot high up into the air. Set in the fire was a huge cauldron filled with a bubbling, poisonous brew.

From time to time, Madge left the dance and peered into the

cauldron, slowly repeating some words of black magic.

Finally, she told her cronies, 'I think it's ready.' She poked her walking stick deep into the big black pot and pulled out a lovely scarf shimmering with many different beautiful colours.

'How beautiful is this poisoned scarf,' she chortled gleefully. 'But whoever wears it will die!'

Madge clutched the scarf to her breast and with the other witches retreated into their cave. The clearing in the woods was empty for a few moments. Then James arrived, pursuing his Sylphide.

As James looked about the glade, the Sylphide suddenly appeared. 'Ah, there you are,' he said in great relief, reaching out to touch the elusive creature. But she slid away, just beyond his grasping hand.

James moved forward. 'Why do you fly away from me?' he asked.

'It's a game,' she answered, with a sweet little laugh. 'Try to catch me.'

James continued to try to capture and hold the Sylphide. But she continued to elude him, darting in and out among the trees. Other sylphides now emerged into the clearing. Soon the entire glade was filled with gracefully leaping and twirling sylphides.

Again and again James turned to take the Sylphide in his arms. But each time she mysteriously slipped from his grasp and in her place stood another sylphide. Then, magically, all the sylphs seems to disappear and James was left alone.

'I'll never succeed in catching the Sylphide,' James moaned in despair. 'What am I to do?'

Suddenly, James saw Madge emerge from her cave. 'What is the matter?' she asked him.

'I came to these woods to find the Sylphide, my true love. But she flies away. She escapes my embraces,' James explained.

'Let me help,' Madge offered, her manner gushing and effusive.

Holding out the brightly coloured scarf in her bony hands, she purred, 'Place this magical scarf around the Sylphide's shoulders. It will not harm her. But it will cause her wings to fall off. The Sylphide

will never escape again. She will be yours forever.'

James gratefully accepted the scarf and the witch disappeared into the shadows.

Attracted by the scarf's brilliant colours, the Sylphide returned. She delicately danced her way to James and kneeled at his feet. Affectionately, he wrapped the scarf around her neck. Delighted at the gift, she arose, embraced him warmly, and kissed him quickly.

A moment later, the Sylphide clutched her heart. Her whole body shook as though in great pain. Her wings separated and drifted away. She stumbled a few steps and sank to the ground. She looked up at James and her gaze showed great fear and horror. Sighing deeply, she breathed her last and died.

The weeping sylphides surrounded their stricken sister. Gently, they raised her limp body into the air and carried her off in their arms.

James sank to the ground in despair. Bitter tears coursed down his face. From within the cave he heard the triumphant laughter of Madge and the other witches. Mingled with these ugly noises were the distant happy sounds of Gurn and Effie's wedding procession.

After a while, Madge came out of the cave. She hobbled over to James, still lying on the ground. Standing over him, she waved her stick exultantly in the air.

Giselle

Hilarion, gamekeeper to the king, stood before the lovely little cottage of the pretty maid, Giselle. He was in love with Giselle and wanted to marry her. But, afraid that she might refuse him, he had long hesitated to propose. Now he stood ready to knock at her door and ask for her hand in marriage.

At that moment he heard someone approaching. Who could that be? he wondered, darting behind some trees to watch.

As Hilarion peered out, he saw the young handsome Prince Albrecht arrive with his squire Wilfrid. Albrecht wore a rich-looking cape over a simple peasant outfit. From his belt hung a sword decorated with the royal crest. Hilarion observed the two men as they walked toward Giselle's cottage.

Wilfrid spoke first. 'Please, master, come away,' he implored. 'Do not go in. Giselle is only a peasant girl. She is not fit for a nobleman like you.'

'Wilfrid, my man,' Albrecht answered, 'leave me be. I love her and she loves me. That is all that matters.'

With that, the Prince threw off his cape and unbuckled his sword. 'Please hide these things, squire, so that I may look like the peasant boy Loys. In this disguise, I have a much better chance of winning Giselle's hand.'

Prince Albrecht, now pretending to be Loys, a common villager, rapped at Giselle's door. Playfully, he ducked out of sight.

Giselle flung open the door and rushed out. Her face was flushed and she looked happy – full of the joy of living.

'Loys? Loys? Is that you?' she called expectantly, looking around in all directions.

From the side of the house came the sound of someone blowing kisses.

'Loys, I know you're there. If you don't come out, I'm leaving,' she threatened.

Albrecht, dressed in his peasant disguise, stepped forward. With open arms he rushed toward the lovely Giselle. Shyly, she ran away. Making believe that she was not glad to see him, she dodged this way and that, trying to escape his hugs and kisses.

Albrecht finally caught her hand and pulled her to a wooden bench. For a long while they sat side by side gazing intently at each other. It was very clear that they were deeply in love. Looking affectionately at her, Albrecht stated solemnly, 'I love you with all my heart and soul. And I promise to be faithful – always.'

Giselle didn't seem to believe him. 'We'll see,' she said as she plucked a daisy from the ground. 'He loves me, he loves me not,' she began laughingly, pulling the petals out, one at a time.

Then, counting ahead to see what the outcome would be, she impulsively flung the flower down and broke into tears. 'The petals do not lie,' she sobbed softly. 'They end with "He loves me not."'

Albrecht picked up the discarded flower. Secretly he pulled off one of the remaining petals and handed the flower back to Giselle. 'Here, my love, try once more,' he urged.

Giselle dried her tears and continued the game. This time, of course, it ended with 'He loves me.'

The two rushed into each other's arms. 'I love you. I love you. I love you,' Albrecht proclaimed enthusiastically.

'I am yours forever,' replied Giselle.

Albrecht dropped to one knee. 'Will you marry me?'

'I will, my dear, I will.' And they hugged and kissed again.

Completely lost in their happiness, the loving couple broke into an exuberant dance that sent them whirling round and round.

Hilarion suddenly sprang from his hiding place. 'Enough of this, he snarled, pushing the two lovers apart. 'I love Giselle and she loves me. You cannot marry her.'

Giselle blushed, then scrutinised her two suitors. She studied one face, then the other. Demurely, she sidled closer to Albrecht. 'I've made my choice,' she quietly announced.

'So, be off with you,' Albrecht ordered.

Hilarion's face turned bright red. He shook his fist in his rival's face. 'You will live to regret your actions,' he vowed passionately. Then he turned and strode angrily away.

After Hilarion departed, the street filled with villagers returning from the grape harvest. Full of good spirits, they skipped and leaped about. Before anyone knew it, the happy crowd began a vigorous peasant dance right in the middle of the street.

'Let's dance,' Giselle begged Albrecht. He quickly agreed, and they were soon doing the energetic steps with the others. The dance grew faster and faster. After a few minutes of high-speed spinning, Giselle staggered and fell to the ground, gasping for breath. Her mother, Berthe, came running out of the cottage. She wiped Giselle's forehead and stroked her face tenderly.

'You really must not dance so much, my dear,' she scolded, knowing that Giselle had a weak heart.

'Please don't worry, Mother,' Giselle said gently. 'I want to dance. Let me join the others, and I will be sure not to get too tired.'

'No, no, my dear,' Berthe insisted, taking Giselle by the hand and pulling her toward the cottage. 'You really must rest now.'

Berthe nudged Giselle inside the little house and closed the door. For a while, Albrecht and the villagers stood and stared sadly at the silent cottage. Then they wandered off.

Meanwhile, Hilarion had found Albrecht's sword where the squire had hidden it. The jealous young man was about to go and show it to Giselle when a horn sounded. It announced the arrival of a royal hunting party, led by the Duke of Courland and his daughter, Princess Bathilde.

Having heard the commotion, Giselle and Berthe came out of their cottage. Impressed at the sight of their elaborately attired visitors, the mother and daughter started preparing refreshments.

Bathilde was charmed by the lovely village maiden who handed her a cool and sparkling drink. 'Tell me about yourself,' she asked Giselle.

Giselle blushed and spoke the first words that sprang to her lips. 'I love a most handsome man. His name is Loys and we are engaged to be married.'

Bathilde took Giselle's hands in her own. 'Imagine that,' she laughed. 'I, too, am betrothed to a very handsome man.' She paused and thoughtfully studied the beautiful Giselle. Then, unclasping the necklace she wore, Bathilde said, 'Here, take this gold chain as my present on your betrothal.'

Giselle gratefully accepted the gift and bowed deeply. As the royal guests returned to the hunt, the villagers resumed their dancing and merrymaking.

Giselle was standing transfixed, touching the chain around her neck, when Albrecht wandered back. He reached for her hand and together they rejoined the gay group. When the dance finally ended, he and Giselle walked off, arm in arm.

Hilarion intervened. 'This man you say you love,' he leered at Giselle, 'is an imposter. Here is his sword. It belongs to a nobleman, not a peasant!'

Albrecht was horror-struck. Furiously, he snatched his sword from Hilarion and lunged at the gamekeeper. But the villagers rushed over and held him back. Dejectedly, Albrecht let the sword fall to the ground.

In a fearful, tremulous voice, Giselle asked Albrecht, 'Is what Hilarion says really so?'

Albrecht could not lie and was unwilling to speak the truth. So he bowed his head and kept silent.

Eyes gleaming, Hilarion now took Albrecht's hunting horn from its hiding place and sounded a long, loud call. In a moment or two, the Duke of Courland and Princess Bathilde returned. The Duke seemed surprised to see Prince Albrecht dressed in peasant clothes.

'Albrecht,' asked the Duke, 'what are you doing here?'

Before Albrecht could answer, Bathilde walked over and took his hand. Turning to Giselle, the Princess said, 'This is the man to whom I'm engaged.'

Realising that Albrecht was not the person she thought he was, Giselle grew extremely flustered. Her whole body began to tremble. She stumbled about, as though in a trance.

'Ohhhh!' she wailed, ripping from her neck the necklace Bathilde had given her.

Then, seeing Albrecht as if for the first time, she moved toward him.

She gaped at him with a puzzled and vacant look. With feeble hands, she bent down and plucked an imaginary flower from the ground. As if playing the same game as before, she removed the invisible petals, one by one. 'He loves me, he loves me not,' she said repeatedly in a hollow voice, nodding her head slowly.

'Poor thing, she has lost her reason,' murmured one villager. 'The shock has driven her mad.'

Suddenly, Giselle interrupted her reverie and began to dance. The steps resembled the gay harvest dance she had performed earlier. But her movements grew increasingly awkward and unbalanced. Finally, she tripped and tumbled down, lifeless. Her soft and lovely form lay there, still and unmoving.

Berthe pressed forward and knelt beside her stricken daughter. Cradling the girl in her arms, she moaned. 'Giselle is dead. My beautiful daughter is gone.'

The grief-stricken Albrecht rushed toward Hilarion and forced him to view the dead girl. Thrusting the gamekeeper's head toward the ground, Albrecht wept, 'See what came of your jealousy. You have killed her.'

Later that night, Hilarion entered the eerie, moonlit forest with some of his companions. He was seeking the grave of his beloved Giselle. In a corner of the woods, he found the fresh mound of dirt and the stone cross that marked her final resting place.

After kneeling and praying, he covered his face with his hands and began to sob. In a short while, his friends, fearing the dark woods, convinced Hilarion to return home.

Right after they left, a veiled figure appeared out of nowhere. She wore a long white dress that glinted in the moonlight. Her name was Myrtha, Queen of the Wilis. Like each Wili, Myrtha was a young maiden who had been engaged to be married, but was betrayed before her wedding day. As Queen, Myrtha made sure that the Wilis, who were doomed to dance from midnight to dawn, returned to their graves on time. Any man who came upon them while they were dancing she sentenced to death.

31

In an imperious voice, Myrtha summoned all the Wilis from their graves. 'Tonight,' she proclaimed, 'we welcome a newcomer, Giselle, to our midst.'

The Wilis watched as Myrtha waved a branch like a magical wand over Giselle's grave. Slowly the earth opened and Giselle stepped out.

The beautiful girl was dressed in white and wore the same veil as the other Wilis. Her eyes were open but glazed over. She looked as though she had been hypnotised. Myrtha signalled Giselle to start dancing.

Wraithlike, Giselle began a dance that grew more and more frenzied. The steps seemed to celebrate her liberation from the grave. As her dance drew to a close, Myrtha heard a sound from the woods. She ordered Giselle to stop and forced the Wilis to follow her into hiding.

Albrecht arrived on the scene, seeking Giselle's tomb. His squire, Wilfrid, followed him. Wilfrid was terror-struck by the ghostly woods and urged his master to leave.

'You go home,' Albrecht ordered the squire. 'I will remain here alone.'

Albrecht kneeled at the grave, absorbed in thought. Suddenly, he caught a glimpse of Giselle. But before he could call out to her, she vanished.

He felt a tap on his shoulder. Spinning around, he saw another vision of Giselle. 'Stay, please,' he implored. But like a puff of smoke she faded away.

The next time Giselle appeared, she was running across the moonlit glade. Now Albrecht caught her tightly in his arms. She struggled free. But her gestures showed him that she wanted to dance.

Together they carried out the steps of a short, impassioned dance. So high did he lift her that she appeared to be floating in air. Merrily, she teased him as in the days gone by. With Giselle in the lead, Albrecht gave chase and they disappeared into the woods.

Meanwhile, Hilarion had returned to the graveside. When the Wilis reappeared, they surrounded him and held him fast. True to their vow to kill any man who came into their midst, they stopped the hapless gamekeeper from escaping.

'Mercy,' he begged. 'Take pity on me.'

'We can show you no more kindness than our law allows,' Myrtha replied sternly.

Bit by bit, the Wilis urged Hilarion forward – toward the lake at the edge of the forest. Once he was at the shore, they cast his body deep into the cold, dark waters.

When the Wilis came back to the clearing, they found Albrecht at Giselle's grave. Now they formed a circle around him. Slowly they inched this intruder toward his death in the lake.

'Spare him,' Giselle begged. 'He never intended to betray me.'

Myrtha showed no sympathy. 'He must perish like the others,' she insisted firmly.

Determined to save his life, Giselle motioned Albrecht to force his way to the cross on her grave. 'It will protect you from Myrtha's power,' she explained.

Albrecht shook his head. 'I will not. I don't want to live without you.'

Myrtha pointed her wand at Giselle and told her to dance. Giselle had no choice but to obey. As Myrtha expected, Albrecht was drawn to dance with her.

'No mortal can keep up with the dancing of a Wili,' Myrtha chortled. 'He will collapse while doing the dance of death.'

Brilliantly, Giselle and Albrecht danced, arm in arm. The hours flew by. Presently, his steps grew weaker. He faltered and sank to the ground.

Giselle continued to dance alone so Albrecht could rest and regain his strength. For a little while, Albrecht just watched Giselle. But the urge to join her became too strong. He rose to his feet, embraced her, and resumed the dance.

Once more, Giselle beseeched Myrtha to let Albrecht live. But Myrtha made it clear she would never allow it.

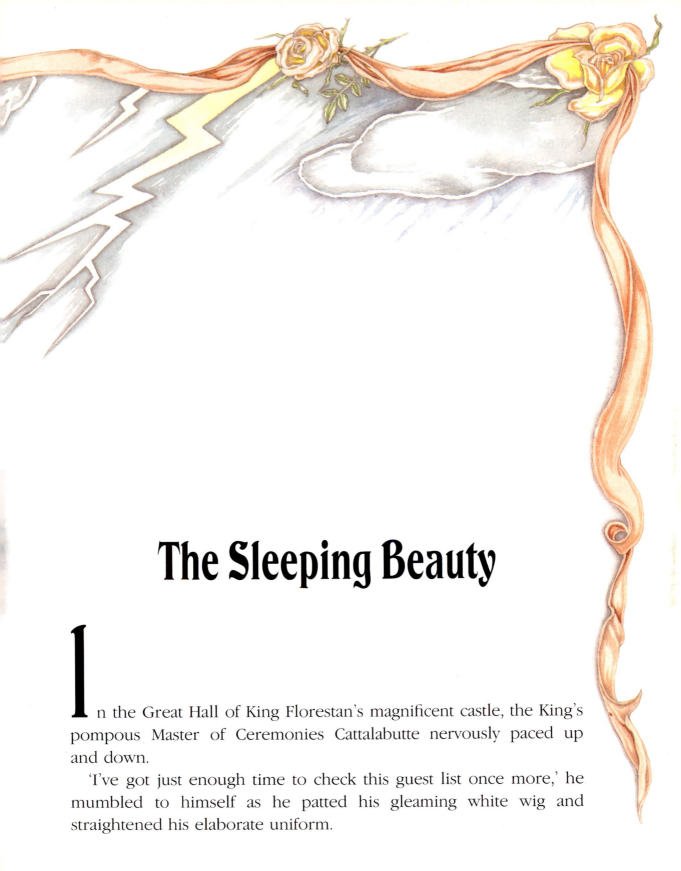

The Sleeping Beauty

In the Great Hall of King Florestan's magnificent castle, the King's pompous Master of Ceremonies Cattalabutte nervously paced up and down.

'I've got just enough time to check this guest list once more,' he mumbled to himself as he patted his gleaming white wig and straightened his elaborate uniform.

37

the fairies were invited – except me. Mistake or not, you're all going to pay.' With that, Carabosse exploded into her fierce cackle, 'Hee, hee, hee.'

Leaning heavily on her walking stick, the gruesome old woman hobbled over to Princess Aurora's cradle. Breathing heavily, she pointed a long, bony finger at the child. In a blood-curdling voice, shrill with anger and venom, she delivered the fateful curse: 'The Princess will grow up. She will become a beautiful Princess – the most beautiful Princess of all. But then, one day, she will prick her finger on a needle.'

Here Carabosse paused. Everyone leaned forward to hear the next words to come from her poisoned lips. 'And she will die! Hee, hee, hee.'

Carabosse's evil oath and dreadful laugh made the Queen go faint with fear and trepidation. As the King tried to comfort his wife, Carabosse clambered back into her coach. With an imperious sweep of her great black cape, she signalled the giant rats to drive her away.

An overwhelming sense of anxiety settled over the gathering. The Lilac Fairy drew near to the despairing royal couple. 'I have not yet delivered my gift,' she reminded them. 'I cannot reverse Carabosse's curse. But I can change it.'

The Lilac Fairy walked to the foot of the cradle and raised her sparkling wand over the sleeping child. Speaking slowly and solemnly, she presented her gift. 'The Princess Aurora will grow up. She will prick her finger on a needle. But she will not die. Instead, she will fall into a deep, deep sleep. The sleep will last for a hundred years. Then, a handsome Prince will awaken her with a kiss. And they will live happily ever after.'

The King and Queen bent their heads humbly before the Lilac Fairy. 'Thank you, thank you,' they said gratefully, 'for the blessing you have bestowed on us and our little baby.'

As soon as the christening was over, King Florestan issued a proclamation: 'No spindles are permitted within one mile of the castle – under penalty of death.'

For years, while the Princess grew up and became ever more beautiful, everyone in the kingdom obeyed the law. The curse of the evil fairy was all but forgotten by the time Aurora turned sixteen.

On that fateful day, the King and Queen decided to hold a most magnificent birthday celebration. In preparation, the palace garden was festooned with flowers and gay decorations.

As the guests began to arrive, Cattalabutte noticed three old hags sitting on the castle lawn spinning cloth with their spindles. The courtier's suspicions were immediately aroused.

'Don't you know that spindles are forbidden here?' he roared, pulling the spindles from their hands. 'Ever since the curse of the wicked Fairy Carabosse, the King has not allowed any spindle within a mile of Princess Aurora.'

'What's the commotion?' asked the King, entering the garden.

The sight of the dreaded spindles made his face cloud over in anger.

'You have broken the law,' he sternly informed the old women. 'The punishment is death by hanging.'

The three hags fell to their knees and began to wail loudly. 'Mercy, mercy,' they cried. 'We meant no harm. We were only spinning our cloth. We beg your forgiveness.'

Strains of joyful melody could now be heard in the garden. The Queen moved toward the King and pleaded with him to spare the three women. 'After all, it is Aurora's birthday,' she said, 'and we don't want anything to mar the occasion.'

The King thought a moment and relented.

As the women scurried away, King Florestan turned to the assembled guests. 'Enough of this unpleasantness. We're here to mark a most joyous event. Let's dance, sing, eat, and be merry!'

A group of brightly dressed peasant girls entered and performed a gay dance using garlands of flowers. Then, the four handsome princes, who had come from England, India, Italy, and Spain to try for Aurora's hand in marriage, wooed her with freshly picked roses. With the party in full swing, other friends of the Princess also danced in her honour.

As the music grew ever more jubilant, the exultant Aurora began a brilliant dance by herself. Near the end, the mounting tempo of the music and the dizzying turns sent her twirling through the throng of clapping guests. As she passed through the crowd, an old woman who was dressed all in black, thrust a gift into Aurora's hand. The gay Princess accepted it without a thought. But the object was a spindle!

The horrified guests reached out to snatch the gift from Aurora's hand. But it was too late. The beautiful Princess had already pricked herself on the spindle's needle! Instantly, Aurora grew weak and slipped to the ground.

Her worried mother and father rushed to her side. Unaware of what had happened, the Princess tried to reassure them. 'Don't worry, dear ones. I will be all right.'

Unsteadily, Aurora rose to her feet and resumed dancing. But the effort proved too much. She reeled from side to side and collapsed into her father's arms.

A terrifying roar of thunder and a gale of hysterical laughter suddenly shattered the terrible silence. The old lady in black emerged from the crowd and revealed herself to be the Fairy Carabosse! 'Hee, hee, hee,' she cackled delightedly. But as the guards dashed forward to capture her, the evil fairy vanished in a puff of smoke.

The guests had gathered around Princess Aurora's unmoving body, lamenting her cruel fate, when the Lilac Fairy appeared. 'Don't despair,' she said consolingly. 'Remember my gift at the christening. Aurora is not really dead. She is just asleep. The spell will last one hundred years.'

Gently and slowly, the Lilac Fairy waved her wand over the assemblage. One by one, the guests closed their eyes and fell into a deep slumber, exactly where they were.

So they remained, fast sleep and unchanged, day after day, year after year. The trees and bushes and vines grew taller and taller until they completely covered the castle. Inside, the networks of cobwebs grew increasingly thick and heavy.

It was exactly one hundred years later when the charming Prince Florimund was out hunting with his friends one day. Growing bored with the hunt, the Prince decided to leave the others and wander through the woods by himself.

Presently, the melancholy Prince came to a lovely lake. So busy was he with his own thoughts that he did not notice the Lilac Fairy float up to the shore in a magical silver boat with filmy sails. It was only after she stepped out that she caught his eye.

'Who are you?' Florimund demanded to know.

'It doesn't matter,' replied the Lilac Fairy. 'What is important is the story I have to tell. Not far from here sleeps a beautiful princess. She has been in a deep slumber for one hundred years. She will only awaken when kissed by a prince who loves her.'

'Who is this enchanted Princess?' Florimund asked incredulously. 'I would very much like to see her.'

Pointing her wand at a dark tree, the Lilac Fairy revealed a vision of Aurora. Struck by her beauty and grace, Prince Florimund stepped forward to touch the Princess. But her image instantly faded away into the shadows from which it had sprung.

'Oh, where has she gone?' moaned Florimund.

'Princess Aurora is across the lake, asleep in the castle. If you want to find her, follow me,' instructed the Lilac Fairy.

The two stepped into the silver boat and glided off across the lake. Alighting on the other shore, they made their way through the dense woods and entered the overgrown castle.

Past sleeping guards and attendants, the wide-eyed Prince and the Lilac Fairy walked until they reached the chamber of the Princess Aurora. There, in the dim light, peacefully resting in her canopied bed, lay the lovely, sleeping beauty.

The Lilac Fairy motioned Prince Florimund forward with her wand. Tenderly, the worthy Prince bent over and gently kissed the lips of the Princess. Slowly she began to stir. Her eyes flutttered open. Taking Florimund's extended hand, she rose from the bed.

Miraculously, the spell was broken. The Great Hall became free of the thickly matted cobwebs. The King and Queen straightened themselves on their thrones. Guards awakened and adjusted their spears. The candles began burning again, and everything looked as splendid as it did before.

Aurora and Florimund entered the Great Hall where the King and Queen presided.

'My dear parents,' Princess Aurora said, 'this is my true love, Florimund. With your permission, we would like to be married.'

'We see your great happiness,' King Florestan said. 'You have our permission and our blessing.'

The King turned to Cattalabutte. 'Tomorrow we celebrate the wedding of our daughter. Draw up the guest list.'

Cattalabutte started to leave. The King called him back. 'And Cattalabutte, pray check the list a thousand times before you send out the invitations!'

'I will, my Lord, believe me I will,' Cattalabutte replied, with a deep bow.

The wedding feast was the most impressive celebration ever held in the magical kingdom. The pompous Cattalabutte, as usual, served as Master of Ceremonies. From his place beside the thrones he announced the names of the illustrious guests: the members of the court, the other royal guests, the fairy godmothers. And, of course, the Lilac Fairy.

Once all the guests had taken their places, the splendidly dressed Princes Aurora and Prince Florimund approached the centre of the hall. Enthusiastically, they opened the festivities with a bubbly, spirited dance. Everyone quickly caught their merry mood. Soon the whole court was dancing in time to the fast-paced music.

King Florestan then joined the happy couple in holy matrimony, and the Lilac Fairy pronounced her special blessing. Finally, the entire gathering kneeled to wish them a long and happy life together.

The Nutcracker

'Wake up, Fritz,' cried Marie excitedly, shaking her sleeping brother. 'Papa has just hung the star on the top branch.'

It was Christmas Eve in the warm, cosy Stahlbaum home a long, long time ago. Since early morning, Marie and Fritz had been wrapping presents, baking biscuits, and making decorations for the party. Towards evening, their parents had gone into the parlour to trim the tree and set out the gifts. And, as was the custom, the children were told to wait in the hall until they were finished. Tired and excited, Marie and Fritz had both fallen asleep.

Marie had awakened first and was peeping through the keyhole in the big doors that led to the parlour. Now Fritz was on his feet, too.

'Move over and let me see,' he said gruffly, nudging Marie out of the way.

'I wish you wouldn't be so pushy,' Marie complained. 'I'd like another look.'

But Fritz would not budge.

Marie turned away. She knew better than to try to win a fight with Fritz. He was two years younger and always had to have his own way. Besides, she wanted nothing to spoil this Christmas Eve party.

A moment later, the first guests began arriving for the celebration, dressed in their finest silks and satins.

'Merry Christmas! Merry Christmas!' they exclaimed, entering in twos and threes. The hall was soon crowded with the aunts and uncles and cousins of the Stahlbaum family – the men bowing to each other and shaking hands, the women hugging and kissing, and the children gaily dashing about.

Suddenly, the Stahlbaum parents flung open the parlour doors and the guests gasped. There stood the most amazing tree! It was glittering with dozens of candles and sparkling with loops of shiny tinsel. Delicious treats hung from every branch – gingerbread men, chocolate soldiers, sugarplums, and long red-and-white candy canes. And stacked at the base were heaps of presents in brightly coloured boxes.

As Marie gazed in awe at the glowing tree, her father handed her a long, slim package. Carefully, she peeled off the wrappings and took out a pair of lovely pink satin ballet shoes. Slipping her feet into the pretty shoes, she tied the shiny ribbons around her ankles.

'Can the dancing begin now?' Marie whispered urgently into her father's ear.

'Of course, my dear,' he said.

But before anything more could be said, Fritz stepped forward. He was wearing the shiny breastplate and helmet he had just received. And he led the boys in a noisy parade of stiff-legged soldiers.

When the boys stopped marching, Marie again asked her father, 'Can we *please* start the dances?'

'Yes,' he replied with a smile. 'Fritz, would you and Marie like to lead?'

Fritz took Marie's hand, and with their cousins, did a dance that looked very much like 'London Bridge Is Falling Down.' The boys and girls were having so much fun that their parents soon joined in. The parlour shook with much laughter and merriment.

All at once, the lights flickered. The room grew silent as everyone exchanged worried glances. Then, very loudly, the huge grandfather clock tolled the hour of nine o'clock. At the same time, the big black owl on top of the clock flapped its dark wings to the strokes of the hour.

The guests froze, alarmed at this curious happening. With the rest of the children, Marie hid behind the grown-ups.

Unexpectedly, the door burst open. A small birdlike man entered the room. Wrapped in a dark, flowing cape, he wore tight black trousers, a short frock coat with cravat and ruffles, and large steel buckles on his shoes. His left eye was covered with a black patch.

A shudder ran through the crowd as the mysterious stranger flitted around the parlour. Marie was the first to recognise him. Of course! It was Herr Drosselmeyer, her godfather and the family's very good friend.

'Herr Drosselmeyer!' she shouted with great delight. 'Herr Drosselmeyer! I'm so glad you're here.' And running over, she flung her arms around his neck.

Marie loved her godfather so very much. She believed there was

'Here,' he said, 'lay the Nutcracker down.'

Tenderly, Marie placed the Nutcracker into the bed and tucked the cover under the white beard. 'Good night, Nutcracker,' she whispered. 'Sleep well. I hope you'll be all better in the morning.'

By now it was getting late. The party was almost over. It was time for the traditional last dance. Marie's godfather directed the slow, stately steps for the grown-ups on one side of the room. And the children, led by Marie and the young Drosselmeyer, danced on the other.

The guests prepared to take their leave. Each one stopped to thank the Stahlbaums on the way out for a most wonderful party. Herr Drosselmeyer and his nephew were the last to go.

For a while, all was quiet in the Stahlbaum house. But when the clock struck midnight, Marie tiptoed down the steps from her bedroom to the parlour. She wore a long white nightgown and slippers. She entered the very dark room, lit only by the candles on the Christmas tree, and crept noiselessly toward the doll's bed.

Very carefully, she picked up the damaged Nutcracker. She hugged it tightly to her chest and held it for a while. Then her eyes felt heavy and she yawned widely. Lying down on the couch with the Nutcracker in her arms, she immediately fell fast asleep.

From out of the shadows, Herr Drosselmeyer suddenly appeared. Without disturbing the sleeping girl, he gently lifted up the Nutcracker. Removing the handkerchief bandage, Drosselmeyer fixed its jaw with a few deft turns of his screwdriver. After setting the Nutcracker back in its bed, the amazing toymaker vanished into the darkness.

Almost at once, the lights on the Christmas tree began to flash on and off, on and off. Marie awakened and jumped up from the couch. In the flickering light she saw Herr Drosselmeyer seated on top of the great clock flapping his arms up and down like a great big owl. She also heard a scurrying sound and saw a big fat mouse scamper across the room. Following him were more mice, all as big as people.

Marie hurried to a hiding place behind the parlour curtain. From there she saw the strangest sight she had ever seen. The Christmas tree began to grow bigger and bigger! Everything under the tree, including the toy soldiers, became life-size. The walls and ceiling of the parlour spread out until Marie could no longer see them in the darkness.

'Oh, my God!' Marie called out. 'What am I to do?'

Marie's eyes fell on the Nutcracker. He had climbed out of his bed and had also grown very tall. Now he stood about a head higher than Marie.

While Marie peered out anxiously, a battle began. A troop of mice, led by the Mouse King, paraded into the room. They kneeled and fired their rifles at the toy soldiers. The frightened soldiers scattered in all directions.

The Nutcracker then stepped in and took command. He formed his troops into lines and signalled for the attack against the mice to begin. The two armies shot at each other; they grappled and tussled. But it was soon clear that the mice were winning.

Marie, frightened by the bad turn of events, urged the Nutcracker and his troops to fight harder. The Nutcracker ordered more weapons and ammunition to be brought in. The men fired big bullets of sweets at the mice. But it was hopeless. More and more soldiers fell in battle, wounded by the mice.

Finally, Marie could bear it no longer. She took off her slipper and flung it with all her might at the Mouse King – hitting him right in the head. He was stunned. Seizing the moment, the Nutcracker ran the mouse through with his sword. The battle was won!

The Nutcracker very proudly pulled the crown off the head of the fallen Mouse King. Solemnly, he placed it on Marie's head. As they looked into each other's eyes, the girl was amazed at what she saw. The Nutcracker had been transformed into a young handsome Prince. And he bore a startling resemblance to Drosselmeyer's young nephew!

Marie stared hard at the familiar, kind face. 'Didn't we just meet at

the Christmas party?' she stammered.

The young Prince didn't reply. He just smiled and bowed low. Then taking Marie's hand, he led her from the parlour into the open air.

Outside, snowflakes were falling in a magical forest.

'Look, look,' Marie called out excitedly. 'The snowflakes are dancing. See how the wind blows them this way and that.'

The Prince put his arm around Marie's shoulders. 'Did you know that the snowflakes are dancing especially for you?' he asked.

Marie and the Prince walked deeper and deeper into the forest, amidst the whirling snowflakes. After a long while, the Prince turned to Marie and said, 'We are approaching a very special place. It's the Kingdom of Sweets.'

'Let's run,' urged Marie, giving the Prince's hand a great tug that almost sent him flying. 'I can't wait to get there.'

Presently, Marie and the Prince entered the enchanted Kingdom to the sound of majestic music.

'It's all too wonderful!' murmured Marie, gazing at all the tempting things made of sugar. But as she stood and gawked at her highly unusual surroundings, a most regal-looking creature approached.

'I am the Sugarplum Fairy,' intoned the gracious lady, leading them to a sugar throne. 'I bid you welcome. Help yourself to the sweets on this tray, while we show you the dances we have prepared for your entertainment.'

Marie trembled with excitement as she and the Prince settled themselves on the throne. 'I have never seen anyone as dazzling as the Sugarplum Fairy,' she marvelled.

The Fairy, attended by a small coterie, shed her stiff, golden outer robes and glided into the centre of the room. She poised gracefully before them in a tutu, the short skirt worn by ballerinas. To the soft strains of the music, she began a light, ethereal, and very dainty dance. The entranced children slid to the edges of their seats and watched delightedly until she had finished.

While the sweets from different lands executed their dances –

Chocolate from Spain, Coffee from Arabia, Tea from China, and Nougat from Russia – Marie longed for only one thing: to see the Sugarplum Fairy once more.

None of the other wonderful dancers could compare with the Fairy. Not the delicate Marzipan Shepherdess, nor the lumbering Mother Ginger, out of whose skirt came the frolicky striped candies, the Polichinelles. Marie was hardly even thrilled by the high point, when the sugar flowers danced the Waltz of the Flowers.

'Please, please let the Sugarplum Fairy dance again,' whispered Marie to the Prince, clasping her hands tightly together.

As though in answer to her prayers, the Sugarplum Fairy emerged. But this time she was not alone. At her side was her gallant Cavalier.

Marie gasped. How surprising, she thought to herself, looking from the Cavalier to her Prince. How close the resemblance. They could almost be the same person.

The music began. The Cavalier bowed deeply and the Fairy obliged with a curtsy and extended her hand. Solemnly at first, and then joyously, they performed the most brilliant and exciting dance that Marie had ever seen.

As Marie watched transfixed, an amazing thing happened. For a moment, she saw herself as the Sugarplum Fairy and her Prince as the Cavalier.

By then it was time for the Prince and Marie to leave the magical kingdom. Stepping into their sleigh, they waved good-bye to their many new friends. As the sleigh silently arose into the sky, Marie cast one misty backward glance.

Before long, Marie was back in the Stahlbaum parlour. She was lying on the couch with the Nutcracker clutched in her arms. Her eyes were open, but they had a puzzled expression. 'Did I just have a glorious dream,' she breathed, 'or did I really have all those splendid adventures?'

Unable to decide, she closed her eyes and soon fell fast asleep. On her face was a smile of the greatest satisfaction.

Swan Lake

When the handsome, young Prince Siegfried arrived at the palace garden to celebrate his twenty-first birthday, the party was already in full swing. From far and wide, his friends had gathered to take part in the festivities.

'Happy birthday! Happy birthday!' they shouted excitedly as he made his way through the crowd.

Siegfried strode over to Benno, his very best friend. 'I'm so glad you could come,' he said, giving his dear companion a warm hug.

'Congratulations to you on this very special day,' exclaimed Benno.

Standing alone at the punch bowl, drinking glass after glass of wine, the Prince saw his old tutor, Wolfgang. Giving the old man a hearty handshake, Siegfried asked, 'How are you, sir?'

Wolfgang obviously had been drinking a bit too much. 'Fine, my boy, just fine,' he said, slurring his words.

The Prince put his arm affectionately around the tutor's shoulders. 'Well, have a wonderful time.'

Siegfried walked towards his seat on the platform. He wanted to enjoy the entertainment that had been arranged in his honour. Once he was seated, peasants from the village appeared in their brightly coloured costumes. With great verve and enthusiasm, they performed a number of their traditional folk dances.

'Excellent! Excellent!' shouted Siegfried when they finished.

'Wolfgang,' he called out to his old friend, 'pour extra wine for these wonderful people.'

The old gentleman filled everyone's glasses and led the crowd of merrymakers in a toast to the Prince's coming of age. The drinking was followed by more dancing and gaiety. All the while, the party kept growing increasingly noisy and raucous.

Suddenly, there was a loud trumpet fanfare. 'The Princess-Mother!' bellowed a palace guard.

With head held high and eyes focused straight ahead, Siegfried's mother strode with great dignity into the garden. She was followed by her four ladies-in-waiting.

Siegfried rose up from his chair and escorted the Princess-Mother to her throne. Although regal-looking in her magnificent purple gown and jeweled crown, his mother's face was set in an angry scowl. The Prince's friends had hidden the wine bottles, but she knew that they had been drinking, and she heartily disapproved.

'Coming of age, my son, is hardly the occasion for indulging in wine and bad behaviour,' she chided.

'Yes, Mother,' he dutifully replied.

SWAN LAKE

The Princess-Mother fixed her stern eyes on Siegfried and continued, 'Today, my son, you are twenty-one years old. You must take on the responsibilities of an adult. It is time to think of choosing a bride. I have planned a ball for tomorrow evening. Six of the most beautiful princesses from the land will be there. And you will select one of them to be your future wife.'

The young Prince's face turned ashen. What if I don't love any of them? he thought to himself.

But the Prince realised that his mother was about to leave and would not be swayed by argument or pleading. So he merely kissed her hand and helped her down from the throne.

On her way out, she directed one final 'Harrumph!' at the birthday celebrants and left the garden.

'Fie!' said Wolfgang as soon as the Princess-Mother was gone. 'Strike up the music! Bring out the wine! Let the dancing resume!'

Soon the rhythmic beat of a spirited polka filled the air. Wolfgang grabbed the hand of a peasant lass and began hopping in time to the music. The faster the tempo, the more vigorously the old man jumped and skipped about. Finally, he fell dizzily to the ground, dragging his young partner down with him. Everyone soon caught the joyous spirit and gaiety returned to the party.

Siegfried tried to enjoy himself. But still he brooded about what the next day held for him.

By now, it was almost evening. Benno noticed the Prince's troubled gaze and wondered how he could distract him. A fluttering of wings and a flock of graceful wild swans flying overhead gave Benno a brilliant idea.

'Siegfried,' Benno called out to his friend. pointing to the swans, 'Let's get our crossbows and follow the birds. We can have a wonderful hunt.'

The Prince was not too enthusiastic, but he agreed to go.

He summoned the servants to bring crossbows and torches for the night-time hunt. Then he and Benno dashed off into the woods with their attendants following.

The hunting party plunged deeper and deeper into the forest until they came to a great silent and silvery lake, gently shimmering in the bright moonlight. The men peered through the leafy treetops for signs of the swans.

Suddenly, the hunters espied the beautiful and slender birds on the lake ahead of them. One particularly beautiful white swan, apparently their queen, led the way.

'Come, my good fellows,' said Benno, pointing into the woods. 'Let's take this path around the lake and await the swans on the other shore.'

Siegfried hesitated. He had seen something move near the water and wanted to get a better look.

'You go ahead,' he urged. 'I'll stay here.'

Siegfried then hid himself among the trees.

As soon as the others were gone, the strangest and most enchanting creature the Prince had ever seen entered the glade. He rubbed his eyes in disbelief. The lovely young woman appeared to be both swan *and* woman. Her dark eyes were set in a pale, lovely face, framed by white swan feathers. On her head glistened a small crown set with diamonds and pearls. The graceful way she rubbed her head against her shoulder reminded him of a swan smoothing its feathers. Yet, at the same time, her poise and bearing seemed very noble and humanlike.

Siegfried was enthralled by the girl's beauty and immediately fell in love with her. He quietly stepped out of his hiding place, hoping not to startle her.

But when she saw him, she became very frightened. Her whole body quivered and fluttered. Waving her graceful arms, she sought to fly away from this apparent danger.

'Please,' begged Siegfried, 'do not flee. I beseech you, stay and speak with me.'

'But – your crossbow . . . ' she said with trembling voice.

'Here, I'll set aside my crossbow,' he said, laying it on the ground. 'I mean you no harm.'

When she had calmed down, Siegfried stepped closer and introduced himself. 'I'm Prince Siegfried. Tell me, who are you? Why are you here?'

Casting her eyes downward, the young woman softly answered, 'I am Odette, Queen of the Swans. I was born a princess in a kingdom far from here. But an evil magician, Von Rotbart, cast a wicked spell. He changed me, and the other princesses of my court, into swans. And he made me Queen of the Swans. Only between the hours of midnight and dawn can I take my human form.'

'How dreadful!' Siegfried fumed. 'Tell me, is there a way to break the spell?'

'It can be done,' replied Odette. 'But it is not easy. Von Rotbart, disguised as an owl, keeps watch all the time. But if a man loves me, marries me, and never loves another, the spell will be broken. I will be a swan no longer.'

The Prince touched his heart with his hand and said tenderly, 'I love you dearly. My only wish is that you love and marry me. By all that is holy, I swear to be faithful to you, and you alone, forever and ever.'

As Siegfried was making his vows, Von Rotbart suddenly appeared. His owl-like face, with its slanty eyes and upturned moustache, was sullen and frowning. Long hair hung from his head and stringy tatters dangled from his clothes. At once mysterious and evil, Von Rotbart slashed the air with his clawlike hands.

Siegfried dropped to one knee, picked up his crossbow, and aimed his weapon at the hideous magician. But before he could release the arrow, Odette ran forward and grabbed his arm.

'Stop, stop,' she begged Siegfried. 'Arrows won't help me. I can only be saved by love.'

Von Rotbart disappeared into the darkness as Siegfried took Odette in his arms and embraced her. Quietly he said to her, 'Tonight, my love you must come to the ball at the castle. It is then that I will be choosing a bride. And I want to select you.'

'How can I come to the ball?' Odette sighed. 'I am a swan, and under Von Rotbart's power until midnight. By the time I arrive, you will already have picked your wife.'

'No power can keep us apart,' Siegfried insisted. 'We will find a way.'

'But Von Rotbart is very clever,' contended Odette. 'He'll do everything he can to keep me from going free. He had many ways to trick you and make you break your promise. If he succeeds, I will die.'

Just then, the other swans, now appearing as pretty young women, came into the lakeside clearing. Following them were Benno and the hunters. Thinking they had finally sighted their quarry, the men stretched their crossbows and prepared to shoot.

'Stop! Don't shoot!' pleaded Odette, flinging herself in front of the swan maidens.

Siegfried stepped out of the shadows. 'Men, lower your crossbows,' he ordered. 'These are not swans. They are princesses under a curse by Von Rotbart, the evil magician.'

The shocked hunters put down their weapons. 'We humbly beg your forgiveness,' they said. 'We didn't know.'

The hunters left just as the first light of dawn was breaking through the darkness. Odette and the swan maidens trembled as the time for departing approached.

'Odette, please, please stay!' cried Siegfried passionately. 'I cannot live without you.'

The Swan Queen answered softly, 'With all my heart I love you and wish I could remain. But I cannot.'

In the mist floating over the lake, the leering owl face of Von Rotbart appeared. His hook-tipped fingers beckoned Odette away from Siegfried. Both Odette and Siegfried struggled desperately to resist the magician, but they were helpless against his evil power. Soon, through the mist, the Prince could see Odette and the other swan maidens silhouetted against the pink dawn sky.

The Princess-Mother's ball was held that evening in the Grand Hall of the castle. Hundreds of gleaming candles cast a warm glow over the magnificently decorated room. The regally clad guests milled about, exchanging excited gossip.

All at once, a line of trumpeters announced the Princess-Mother and Siegfried. The two approached the ballroom and advanced to their thronelike seats on the raised platform.

But Siegfried's thoughts were far away. He was thinking only of Odette.

Noting the distant look on his face, the Princess-Mother upbraided him. 'What is the matter with you? Pay attention to our guests. Remember your duties as Prince!'

Siegfried nodded and pretended to watch. The herald announced the names of the arriving guests. Last to come were the six princesses from whom Siegfried was to pick his bride. The young women performed a stately waltz to exhibit their beauty and grace.

When the dance was over, the Princess-Mother tapped his arm sharply with her fan. 'You must now dance with each of the girls. Go on, go on.'

Dutifully Siegfried rose from his throne and woodenly danced, in turn, with the six young women.

'All right then,' the Princess-Mother eagerly asked when he returned, 'which one will it be? Who is to be your bride?'

The image of Odette shone clearly before his eyes. Siegfried could not bear the thought of marrying anyone else. 'I am sorry, mother,' he murmured. 'I will not – or rather – I cannot marry any of them.'

The Princess-Mother flushed angrily and glared at him. 'Do you dare to disobey me?' she challenged.

Before Siegfried could answer, the herald rushed over to the Princess-Mother. 'A strange-looking couple has just arrived,' he announced breathlessly. 'A tall, bearded knight who appears to be of great wealth and station and his beautiful daughter.'

'Well, bring them in, bring them in,' the Princess-Mother ordered.

Everyone turned to gaze at the mysterious twosome – the resplendent knight and his strikingly attractive companion. Both were dressed entirely in black. The knight introduced his daughter as Odile.

Siegfried was staggered at the sight of the beautiful girl. 'Why – why it's Odette!' he gasped.

At this moment, Siegfried did not see the ghostly vision that appeared in the shadows. It was the true Odette come to warn Siegfried that the knight was really Von Rotbart and the girl, Odile, his daughter.

Mistaking the black-garbed girl for his beloved Odette, the Prince stepped down and took her hand in his. 'I knew our love would not be denied,' he whispered in her ear. Odile smiled slyly.

The Princess-Mother was so delighted to see Siegfried's interest in the attractive young woman that she invited the knight to join her on the platform. 'Let the entertainment begin,' she commanded.

First, guests from Spain, Hungary, and Poland did their brilliant native dances. Then Siegfried and Odile stepped forward. Believing that he had Odette in his arms, the Prince danced with movements of great joy, warmth and affection. So blinded was he by love that he did not notice how Odile differed from Odette. The imposter moved with small, tight steps and used wooden stilted gestures that showed her icy cold character.

As their dance came to a close, the love-struck Siegfried bowed before the knight and asked for his daughter's hand in marriage. The knight grinned maliciously. 'Of course, my son,' he replied at once. 'There is, though, one condition. You must swear to be eternally loyal.'

Siegfried remembered that he had taken that oath once before. He hesitated for a moment. Why should I have to pledge my love again? he wondered. But so sure was he that Odile and Odette were the same person, that he uttered the fateful words.

All at once a cold wind ripped through the Great Hall. The candles blew out, plunging the huge room into darkness. The frightened guests fled. Crashes of thunder shook the mighty timbers of the castle. Stabbing flashes of lightning cast their bright beams.

The flickering gleams of light revealed the knight and his daughter

Once more, Swanilda smiled and waved at the pretty girl in the window. But still the girl just sat there, stiff and unmoving. She appeared completely absorbed in the book she always seemed to be reading.

The girl's name was Coppélia. Swanilda had heard that she was the daughter of Dr Coppélius, the mysterious scientist who was said to have special magical powers. While everyone in the village had seen her at the window, no one had ever spoken to her.

Swanilda had two reasons to be angry with Coppélia. Not only had Coppélia snubbed Swanilda's greeting, but she suspected that the girl in the window had flirted with Swanilda's boyfriend, Franz.

Suddenly, Swanilda glimpsed Franz entering the square. She darted into a dark space between two buildings. From this hiding place, she watched the brightly dressed Franz cross the square with a jaunty step. Approaching Dr Coppélius's house, the young man glanced around furtively. Believing that he was alone, he put hands to his lips and blew Coppélia a kiss.

At first Coppélia ignored Franz, just as she had Swanilda. But then, slowly and jerkily, she rose from her seat and bowed deeply to the admiring Franz.

Franz was delighted that Coppélia had noticed him. He clapped his hands and jumped into the air to show his pleasure. But a moment later, his smile froze. He guiltily turned to look at Swanilda's house on the other side of the square. After all, he was betrothed to Swanilda. Was he also in love with Coppélia? Which girl should he choose?

While he was trying to sort out his true feelings, the curtains of Coppélia's window were pulled closed. The girl disappeared from sight. Somewhat embarrassed, Franz continued to stare at the empty window. So preoccupied was he, that he didn't notice Swanilda standing right behind him.

'You scoundrel!' Swanilda shouted. 'You cad! You're willing to leave me for a girl you have only seen in a window. Shame on you, shame, shame. I hate you, Franz. I never want to see you again!'

'My dearest,' Franz began, reaching his arms out to Swanilda. 'You are my only love. Coppélia means nothing to me.'

'Don't tell me that,' said Swanilda bursting into tears. 'I don't believe you.' And she turned and stalked away, every step echoing off the rounded stones of the empty village square.

A number of townspeople now began to fill the square and to dance happily in the bright sunshine. Swanilda came back and, avoiding Franz, joined a group of her friends in the crowd.

Soon the town burgomaster entered and called for attention. When everyone had quietened down, he made his announcement: 'The lord of the manor has decided to give our town a great new bell. You are all invited to the festival tomorrow when he will present his magnificent gift. To make the occasion even more special, the gracious lord will marry any couples already engaged and will give generous dowries to the lucky newlyweds.'

'Swanilda,' the burgomaster continued, smiling broadly, 'I assume that you and Franz will be the first couple to be married.'

Swanilda remained quiet. She didn't know if she wanted to marry Franz or not. The burgomaster looked terribly disappointed.

'I – I – I just can't say,' Swanilda stammered.

'Perhaps I can help you make up your mind,' the burgomaster offered, pulling a large ear of wheat from his jacket pocket. 'Take this ear of wheat and shake it near your ear. If you hear something, your lover loves you truly. If you hear nothing, your lover cares for another.'

Hesitatingly, Swanilda accepted the ear of wheat. Staring at Franz's face in the crowd, she shook the stalk back and forth. The villagers all strained to listen.

'I hear – I hear . . . ' Swanilda paused, 'I hear nothing!' Flinging the straw to the ground, she sobbed, 'Our engagement is over!'

'Women . . . ' mumbled Franz, tossing woeful glances at Swanilda over his shoulder as he left the square.

The crowd soon returned to their joyful mood. All sang and danced in anticipation of the coming celebration.

After a while, Dr Coppélius pushed open the door to his house. Out stepped the doddering old man, dressed in a black flowing cape, with unruly grey hair sticking out on all sides of his head. He closed the door very firmly behind him and turned a big, heavy key in the lock. Having tried the door several times to make sure that it was securely fastened, Dr Coppélius leaned hard on his cane and headed across the square.

Some young men, seeing Dr Coppélius, ran forward and pulled on his coat tails. They urged him to dance with them. 'No, no,' he protested. 'I'm too old for such frivolity. Leave me be. I have many more important things to do.'

But the playful merrymakers would not let him go. They jostled and twirled the old man until he became quite dizzy. In the midst of the scuffle, his key fell out of his pocket. Neither the old man nor the dancers noticed, though, and they all marched off to the tavern.

The square stood empty until Swanilda and her friends entered on their way to supper. Swanilda spotted the key lying there and picked it up. 'There's only one door this key will fit,' she declared emphatically. 'Follow me.' So saying, Swanilda led her small group across the square to the house of Dr Coppélius. Slowly and carefully she slipped the key into the lock and opened the door.

'What luck!' she squealed with delight. 'Now I'll finally be able to have a word or two with Coppélia.'

'Oh, you shouldn't do that,' one of her friends warned. 'What if you're caught?'

'Don't be a silly goose,' Swanilda assured her.

Very frightened, but too curious to stay behind, the girls followed Swanilda as she stealthily crept into the large, dark interior of Dr Coppélius's house.

Just then, Franz appeared in the deserted square carrying a tall ladder. 'If Swanilda won't have me,' he said aloud to himself, 'then I'll plead my love for Coppélia.'

Franz leaned his ladder against the balcony of Dr Coppélius's house. He was about halfway up when the doctor returned, having just discovered that his key was missing. Seeing Franz on the ladder, the dotty old scientist cried out, 'Hey, what are you doing there?'

Quickly, Franz scampered down, grabbed the ladder, and ran for his life. The old man, waving his stick threateningly in the air, gave chase, but could not overtake the young fellow.

With Franz gone, Dr Coppélius got down on his hands and knees to hunt for his lost key. As he searched around, he noticed that the door to his house was wide open. Rising unsteadily to his feet, he hurried inside as nimbly as he could.

Meanwhile, Swanilda and her friends were amazed at what they had found inside. Scattered about were a number of life-size dolls! Each one was dressed in a different costume and seemed to be frozen in a set position. Here sat one with both arms raised. There stood a figure poised on one leg.

The girls were startled by these strange dolls, but they were also filled with curiosity and rushed about touching each one.

'I wonder what this is for?' one girl asked, noticing a big red button on the wall. She pushed it without waiting for an answer. In an instant, the dolls seemed to come to life. With short, abrupt mechanical movements, they moved and danced about, making the girls giggle with delight.

While her friends played with the dolls, Swanilda moved toward the curtained window alcove, looking for her rival in love. She cautiously pulled back the curtain and saw Coppélia. Politely Swanilda curtsied deeply to the seated figure. 'Good evening, Coppélia,' she said. But Coppélia did not look up. She sat quietly with the book in her hand.

Swanilda was confused. She stepped forward and tapped Coppélia lightly on the shoulder. No response.

Growing even braver, Swanilda bent over and snatched the book from Coppélia's hands. Coppélia did not move.

Approaching still closer, Swanilda put her hand on Coppélia's chest

to feel for a heartbeat. There was none.

'She's not a girl at all!' Swanilda shouted. 'She's just a doll like all the others.'

In a moment, Swanilda was doubled over with laughter. 'Just think,' she gasped, 'Franz fell in love with a doll!'

Boldly strutting around the room, Swanilda imitated the automatic steps and hand movements of the mechanical dolls.

At that moment, Dr Coppélius came storming into the room. Shaking his walking stick, he drove the girls down the stairs. Then he ran from doll to doll to make sure they had not been broken.

Finally, he went to the curtain corner to see that his favourite doll, Coppélia, was safe. Satisfied that she was, he drew the curtain. Little did he know that Swanilda was hiding in the corner.

But now Dr Coppélius heard a noise at one of the windows. It was Franz, who had come back to see Coppélia. The doctor watched as Franz climbed off the ladder and stepped through the window into the room.

'Ah-hah,' Dr Coppélius shouted as he lunged toward Franz. 'Now I've got you.'

'Wait, wait,' Franz begged, fleeing the wild swings of Dr Coppélius's walking stick, 'I've come to declare my love for the beautiful Coppélia.'

Dr Coppélius hesitated. Then a false, forced smile crossed his face as he got an idea. 'That's different,' he said, his voice dripping with sweetness. 'Come in, come in. Join me for a drink.'

The dollmaker poured two drinks. But when Franz turned away for an instant, the old man added a powerful sleeping potion to the lad's glass. After only two sips, Franz's head began to nod. A minute later, he slipped from the chair and fell fast asleep on the floor.

Meanwhile, Swanilda had removed Coppélia from her chair and tossed the lifeless doll to one side. She put on the dress that the doll had been wearing and sat in Coppélia's chair.

Having taken care of Franz, Dr Coppélius pulled aside the curtains to look at his lovely Coppélia. Not realising that this was Swanilda, he wheeled her into the centre of the room. Convinced that his doll was as beautiful as ever, Dr Coppélius took down a large, heavy dusty volume of magical spells from the top shelf of his bookcase. He leafed through the pages, seeking a formula that would transfer part of Franz's life force to Coppélia so that she would come alive.

'Ah-hah!' exclaimed Dr Coppélius. 'Here it is!'

With his eyes fixed on the open book, he walked over to Franz and waved his hands over the young man, head to toe. Then, believing he held Franz's life force in his hands, the old sorcerer dashed over to the disguised Swanilda, opened his hands, and showered the spirit of life over her body.

Swanilda now decided to have some fun with Dr Coppélius. She made believe that the magic was working. Slowly, she began to stir, one part of her body at a time. Stiffly, she raised one arm then the other. Then she jerked herself up, but collapsed at the waist so that she was doubled over. Finally, she started to walk, step by step, lurching from side to side like a drunken soldier on parade.

Dr Coppélius could hardly believe his eyes. Astounded at the effects of his magic, he tried to teach the 'doll' new tricks. At Coppélius's command, Swanilda moved in all different ways and performed one brilliant dance after another.

But in time, the girl lost interest in following Dr Coppélius's directions. She walked over to Franz and rolled him over with her foot. With a powerful kick, she sent the magic book flying across the room. Running wildly around the room, she attacked the other dolls with the doctor's walking stick.

The frenzied Coppélius tried to get her to stop. Afraid that she would hurt herself as well as the others, he plopped her down in the chair. Then, shaking his finger at her, he rolled the chair back to its place behind the curtains.

By then the sun was up and Franz was stirring. When he was fully awake, Dr Coppélius ordered him to leave. Franz did not have to be

asked twice. In a second, he had backed out of the window and run away.

Dr Coppélius now heard some strange noises from behind the curtain. He rushed over and flung back the drapes. To his dismay, he saw his exquisite Coppélia hanging limply over the chair.

'Woe is me!' cried Dr Coppélius, holding his greying head in his hands. 'My dream of turning dolls into humans was only that – a dream.'

Swanilda, who had been hiding in the drapes, slipped out without being seen by Dr Coppélius. She fled from the house and bounded down the street to catch Franz.

'Franz, Franz,' she called out.

At the sound of her voice, he turned and ran towards her. The two lovers met in a passionate embrace.

'Can you ever forgive me?' Franz asked in a quavering voice, not knowing what Swanilda had just witnessed.

'Of course, my love. You are the only one for me,' she answered as, hand in hand, they crossed the town square.

The next day was the festival. The villagers gathered on the great lawn of the manor house to celebrate the blessing of the bell by the lord of the manor. Swanilda and Franz, and the other couples who were about to be married, looked magnificent in their finely embroidered new clothes. In grand style, the lord of the manor offered congratulations and presented them with their dowries.

In the midst of the gaiety, Dr Coppélius pushed his way through the crowd. 'It isn't fair!' he shouted. 'All my dolls are ruined. I now realise that Swanilda and Franz played me for a fool. What do I get for all my loss and suffering?'

'Go away, you silly old man,' shouted one villager. 'It's your own fault.'

But Swanilda came to his defence. 'You're quite right, Dr Coppélius,' she insisted above the noisy cries. 'Here is my dowry. Maybe it will help ease the pain we caused you.'

Dr Coppélius was about to accept the money from Swanilda when the lord of the manor stepped forward. 'My good man, take instead this bag of gold to compensate you. The dowry is for Swanilda and Franz.'

With that, the happy couple were wed. Franz offered Swanilda his hand, and they danced together. As the musicians played one merry tune after another, the townspeople all joined in. One glance at the beaming faces of Swanilda and Franz told everyone that out of their disagreement had come an even stronger love.

Romeo and Juliet

It was the beginning of a bright new day in the Italian city of Verona, a long time ago. The large central market-place was slowly filling up with people arriving from all parts of the city. Shopkeepers were unlocking their doors and raising their window blinds. Farmers from the countryside were unpacking their fruits and vegetables. And servants were milling about, waiting to buy provisions for their masters.

Two footmen from the wealthy house of Montague started to cross the square. A coachman and butler from the equally distinguished house of Capulet approached them from the opposite direction.

The Montagues and Capulets were two families of Verona who had once quarrelled and had remained enemies since then. So great was their enmity that it had infected the people who worked for them as well.

As they passed each other, one of the Montague servants muttered something unpleasant under his breath.

A Capulet servant grabbed him by the shoulder. 'What did you say?' he demanded to know.

'None of your business.'

'Well, I'm making it my business.'

No one knew who pushed whom or who was the first to draw a sword. But in a few minutes the entire market-place erupted into a violent sword fight as members from each of the dynasties entered the fray.

Attracted by the commotion, the heads of the two houses – Lord Montague and Lord Capulet – came into the square. With swords held high, they rushed to join the struggle.

Finally, into the square marched the Prince of Verona. In an imperious voice that easily rose above the hubbub, he commanded, 'Halt this fighting at once.'

Not daring to disobey the Prince, the combatants of both families sheathed their swords and left the market-place.

Back in Lord Capulet's castle, Juliet, his beautiful fourteen-year-old daughter, was playing hide-and-seek with her nurse. On his return, Lord Capulet and his wife entered her room and interrupted the game.

'We've got some wonderful news for you,' Lady Capulet informed her daughter. 'The young noble, Paris, has asked for your hand in marriage. And we have agreed. We will present him to you at tonight's masked ball.'

'But, Mother,' Juliet protested, 'I am too young to be married.'

'It's all arranged, my dear,' Lord Capulet answered for his wife. 'You'll find that he is very handsome – and very wealthy, too. It will be a good match.'

Juliet sat quietly and absorbed the news. 'As you like, Father,' Juliet agreed weakly.

All of Verona's leading citizens – except the Montagues – arrived at the Capulets' house for the ball that evening. The guests danced to the gay music, amidst much eating, drinking, and loud chatter.

The party was in full swing when Romeo, son of the house of Montague, walked past the castle gates with his two mischievous friends, Mercutio and Benvolio. He was attracted by the sound of the music and merrymaking. 'It sounds like they're having a good time,' Romeo said wistfully.

Mercutio got a devilish twinkle in his eye and said, 'Let's go to the Capulet celebration. Since it is a masked ball, we'll wear disguises. No one will recognise us as Montagues.'

'Splendid thought!' Romeo readily asserted.

With that, the three young men donned masks and slipped boldly into the Capulet house.

Romeo and his friends entered the ballroom at a particularly festive moment. The lordly Paris had just been presented to Juliet, and the two were having their first dance together. But as Juliet turned on Paris's arm, her eyes met those of the dashing Romeo. At that instant, a very special bond was forged between the two.

Juliet was struck by the rugged good looks of the tall, dark stranger. His proud and noble bearing bespoke great boldness and strength. Yet his gleaming eyes shone with warmth and tenderness.

In that same fleeting moment, Romeo grew faint with love. Juliet appeared to be a vision of loveliness. I never saw true beauty till this night, he thought to himself, his eyes riveted on her lithe and graceful figure.

Enchanted by the lovely girl and eager to know her better, Romeo began to make his way towards her. Paris, noting Juliet's obvious interest in the masked stranger, moved across to learn the young man's identity.

Mercutio realised at once that this could be dangerous. Should Paris discover that the masked man was a Montague, blood would surely be shed. So Mercutio bounded into the centre of the room and launched into a wild dance. The especially vigorous steps distracted the guests and captured their attention. Everyone, including Paris, was captivated, and the tense moment passed.

But then Tybalt, Juliet's hot-blooded cousin, noticed the unfamiliar, though masked, intruder. He edged his way closer to Romeo and eavesdropped on his conversation. After a few words, Tybalt, the loyal Capulet, exclaimed loudly, 'I know that voice. It is Romeo, a Montague. He is here to mock us.'

A hush fell over the ball as Tybalt drew his sword. 'Prepare to defend yourself,' he hissed at Romeo.

Lord Capulet stepped between them. 'Put away your weapon, Tybalt,' he ordered. 'The gentleman has done us no wrong. And he is a guest in our house. There will be no fighting here.'

Tybalt bowed low. 'I am your servant, my lord.'

The anger was gone now. But so was the gaiety and sparkle of the ball. The hosts kissed Juliet good night and retired to their chamber. Juliet climbed the stairs to her bedroom. As she prepared for bed, she could think only of Romeo. So full was her heart with love for him that she could not sleep. She wandered out to the balcony overlooking the garden.

Romeo, also restless out of his love for Juliet, decided to come to the Capulet garden, just to be a little closer to his beloved. Juliet had no knowledge that he was there. Believing that she was alone, Juliet expressed aloud her feelings for Romeo. She spoke of her fear that their families would keep them apart.

'Oh, Romeo,' she declared finally. 'What do I care that you are a Montague? I think only about the person that you are. More than any other, you stir my heart with the greatest desire.'

Romeo was startled to hear Juliet's confession. Stepping into the moonlight where she could see him, he said, 'Fair Juliet, my soul trembles at the sound of your voice. I love you more than words alone can say.'

'Oh, my Romeo. How happy you make me.'

Made bold by her response, Romeo said earnestly, 'Entrust yourself to me, Juliet, and I will shelter and care for you always.'

'I place all faith and hope in you, my love,' Juliet responded softly, 'but I fear for your safety. If my kinsmen find you here, they will surely kill you.'

'My love for you will be my shield and protector. Your assurance and certainty fills me with strength and spirit.'

Then, sinking to one knee and placing his hands over his heart, Romeo solemnly asked, 'My own true love, will you consent to be my wife?'

Juliet's heart leapt with excitement. She started to speak but heard footsteps and held back the words. 'The answer must wait. My nurse is stirring and I must go. Tomorrow I will send a note. For now, a thousand kisses good night.'

'Good night, sleep well. Until tomorrow!'

Romeo watched Juliet leave the balcony and enter her room. 'Adieu,' he answered her, as he turned and disappeared into the shadows of the garden.

On the next day, there was a festival in Verona. The market-place was thronged with celebrating townspeople. Juliet's nurse forced her way through the crowd. 'Has anyone seen Romeo?' she kept asking as she picked her way past vendors and shoppers.

No one knew of Romeo's whereabouts. Finally, the nurse noticed him entering the square. She hurried to catch up with him.

'Here,' she said breathlessly on reaching him, 'is a letter from Juliet.'

Romeo thanked the nurse and quickly tore open the paper.

'She loves me! She loves me!' he exulted. 'And she has consented to be my wife. She says that we should meet at Friar Laurence's cell, and there be secretly married.' Romeo twirled round ecstatically. 'Surely there is no man happier than I!'

With a quick hug for the nurse, Romeo hastened away to the cell of Friar Laurence.

When Romeo arrived, the priest was seated alone, contemplating a basket filled with flowers from which he planned to prepare some medicines. He turned to make Romeo welcome.

'Hello, my son. What can I do for you?' the Friar asked, motioning for Romeo to be seated.

'Oh, Friar, sir. I've just met the most enchanting girl in the world. And I want you to marry us.'

The Friar studied the face of the eager and expectant young man before him. 'Well,' he said slowly, 'tell me. Who is your bride to be?'

'The greatest treasure in all Verona – Juliet.'

The Friar stood up and walked around his bare-walled cell. 'But she's a Capulet,' he said huskily. 'And you're a Montague . . .'

'That's why the marriage must be done now and why it must be kept secret.'

'I see, I see,' Friar Laurence murmured thoughtfully. For some time the good man carefully considered the situation.

After a while, he told Romeo, 'It is not for us to question the mysterious happenings in the universe. Perhaps this is God's way to reconcile the two families. Yes, I will join you and Juliet in holy matrimony.'

Romeo bent his head in gratitude. Silently, he and the Friar, each occupied with his own thoughts, awaited Juliet's arrival.

Moments later, she hastened in. Romeo and Juliet knelt before the Friar, as he pronounced the sacred words of the marriage ceremony over their bowed heads. To the final words he added this fervent wish: 'May God grant that this union will end the strife between the Montagues and the Capulets.'

Juliet returned home with her nurse while Romeo started back alone. On the way, he passed through the market-place, still filled with

sleep, even for a short while, fills me with dread. But I will take your sleeping potion. Come what may, I must be with my Romeo.'

Juliet returned to the castle. To avoid suspicion, she informed her parents that she was now willing to marry Paris. Lord and Lady Capulet rejoiced. 'Tomorrow we shall celebrate this joyous event,' her father said smilingly.

Back in her bedroom, Juliet delayed taking the sleeping potion. But finally, deciding it was the only way to join Romeo, she drank the special drink that Friar Laurence had prepared. She laid her head on the pillow and passed into a deep slumber.

In the morning, Juliet's parents, along with Paris, came to her bedroom eager to start the wedding preparations. They tried to wake Juliet, but she did not stir.

'Nurse, nurse,' Juliet's mother ordered. 'Come here and help us to rouse the child.'

The nurse hastened over to the bedside and peered into Juliet's glazed eyes. 'Oh my God,' she cried, 'our Juliet is dead!'

The Capulets gathered around Juliet's bed to grieve over this great calamity. The nurse and mother moaned and wept pitifully. Lord Capulet held his head in his hands and wailed, 'Why, oh why, has our beloved Juliet been taken from us?'

His face drawn with anguish, he instructed that Juliet be placed in the family vault. 'I cannot bear to contemplate life without her song and laughter,' he lamented pitifully, as her body was borne away.

Meanwhile, Romeo's exile had taken him to Mantua. Sorrowfully, he wandered the streets, lost and forlorn without his true love.

Presently, Romeo's servant arrived from Verona. Having overtaken Friar Laurence's messenger, this servant had reached Romeo first. 'Juliet is dead,' he mistakenly informed Romeo. 'And her body has already been moved to the Capulet crypt.'

Romeo sank to the ground, stunned by the horrible news. 'Oh, the pain and misery of it all,' he exclaimed, overcome for a long while with shock and dismay. 'Gone is the love of my life. Gone, too, is all beauty, hope, desire, and joy from the world. Only death can put an end to my suffering. Only death can restore my beloved to me.'

The distraught lover paced nervously back and forth. 'How can I remain here in Mantua – so far from my Juliet?' he cried. 'If I could not be with her in life, at least I shall be with her in death.'

Despite the danger of capture, Romeo sped back to Verona and descended the steps to the dark Capulet crypt. When he arrived, he found Paris there, grieving for Juliet.

Paris recognised Romeo and barred his entrance into the crypt. 'You murdered Tybalt,' charged Paris, blocking the way with outstretched arms. 'So terrible was Juliet's despair at losing her cousin, she no longer wished to live.'

Romeo tried to push past Paris. 'Do not try to stop me from entering. I warn you, I am a desperate man and I will not hesitate to harm you.'

'I will not let you proceed any farther,' insisted Paris.

As their words grew more heated, the young men drew their swords. They fought a duel until Paris fell, killed by Romeo's sharp blade.

Laying Paris gently aside, Romeo approached the vault where Juliet lay sleeping. He bent over her limpid form, kissed her lips, and made this pledge: 'Fair one, I vow never to leave you again. Here will I remain with you until the end of time.'

From a pocket deep within his cloak, Romeo withdrew a vial of poison. 'To my love,' he said. Then, casting a final adoring look at Juliet, he swallowed the draught in one gulp. With a massive shudder, the stalwart Romeo fell to the crypt floor and died.

When Juliet awoke from her long sleep, shivering in the cold crypt, she espied Romeo. Happy that the Friar's plan had worked so well, she mused, 'Oh, Romeo's probably asleep as I have been.'

Bending over, she gently shook the still figure. 'Wake up, dear Romeo, wake up.'

The handsome lad remained rigid and unmoving. 'Oh, Lord,' she

cried out, 'he's dead! Cruel, cruel fate,' she moaned. 'I have lost that which I wanted more than anything else in the whole world.'

Moving now with fierce determination, Juliet pulled Romeo's dagger from its scabbard. Without a moment's hesitation, she plunged it into her breast. Her body fell across that of her beloved.

The two lifeless lovers were found a little while later by their sorrowing families, the Capulets and the Montagues. The Prince of Verona soon arrived and addressed these remarks to the two heads: 'See what horror your hate has spawned. Your kinsmen, Mercutio, Tybalt, and Paris lay dead. Your children, Romeo and Juliet, have ended their young lives. When will this scourge end?'

Lord Capulet reached out to Lord Montague. 'Give me your hand, sir. Let us put an end to that which has caused us both much pain.'

'Indeed, let the sacrifice of our children mark the end of our enmity.'

'It is a gloomy peace that we have achieved,' commented the Prince. 'For never was there a story of more woe than this of Juliet and her Romeo.'

Beautiful young Cinderella had been watching her two stepsisters from her place at the fire. She was miserably dressed in a torn frock and a shabby apron, but even in this simple attire, she possessed exquisite beauty. Forgetting the lowly position she had since her father remarried, Cinderella picked up one piece of the scarf and put it over her shoulders. Delighted by the luxurious feel of the fabric, she did a little dance with the scarf. She imagined that she, too, had been invited to the ball. A handsome young man had asked her to dance. Together they twirled around and around the elegant ballroom.

Just then her stepsisters entered. 'Don't give yourself any fancy airs,' Zlyuka ordered angrily, plucking the scrap of silk away from Cinderella. 'Such fine fabric looks ridiculous with your tattered clothes and dirty face.'

While the sisters were scolding Cinderella, there came a knock at the door. Cinderella let in an old, hunchbacked woman leaning on a crooked walking stick and dressed in the most ragged clothes.

'Alms for the poor,' the old woman begged in a high, cracking voice.

'Tell her to go away,' shouted Krivlyaka. 'We're too busy.'

'Yes, we're too busy,' echoed Zlyuka.

Cinderella moved close to the beggar-woman. 'I'm sorry that I don't have money to give you,' she whispered gently. 'But here is a crust of bread from my dinner.'

'Bless you, my child,' the woman said, taking the bread.

As she made her way out, some tradespeople arrived to prepare the sisters for the ball. The dressmaker brought two elegant gowns, and the shoemaker carried in two pairs of shiny satin shoes. The two women struggled and strained to fit into their tight dresses and pointed shoes.

Next, the hairdresser carefully combed and set each sister's wispy hair and sprayed each coiffure in place. And the jeweler carefully adjusted their diamond necklaces and bracelets.

The dancing master, meanwhile, had been waiting patiently. When he saw that the sisters were dressed and coiffed, he reviewed the steps he had taught them. Noisily, the two clumsy women waddled through the dances they would be doing at the ball. Stiff and awkward, they showed an amazing lack of grace.

Finally, it was time for the stepsisters to leave for the ball. They said not a word to Cinderella as they departed, leaving the poor girl sitting all alone in front of the hearth.

For a while, Cinderella gazed intently at the portrait of her dear mother over the fireplace. Presently, she began to imagine that she was at the ball. She took the broom and pretended it was a handsome prince who had asked her to dance. Then, broom in hand, she danced flawlessly, performing with grace the steps her sisters had struggled to master.

While Cinderella was spinning and whirling, the old beggar-woman suddenly reappeared. Cinderella jumped back with a start because, before her eyes, the woman became transformed into a beautiful fairy, dressed entirely in white.

'Come, come, Cinderella, don't just stand there staring,' the fairy said to her. 'It's late already. If you're to go to the ball, you have to get ready.'

Cinderella's eyes opened wide. 'The ball?' she asked incredulously. 'Who are you? And why have you come?'

'I'm your Fairy Godmother. And I've come to make your dreams come true because of your kindness. Hurry, now. We've got to replace your rags with fine clothes.'

With that, the Fairy Godmother waved her wand through the air. In a flash, four more fairies appeared. 'These fairies are my helpers,' the Godmother explained. 'They are named after the four seasons – Spring, Summer, Autumn, and Winter.'

Each fairy curtsied low to Cinderella. Then they got to work. From thin air the Fairy of Spring produced a thin and filmy white gown, as light as the wind. Summer brought Cinderella lovely roses to decorate her lovely, long hair. Autumn presented the girl with a splendid cloak

Suddenly – and to her surprise – the clock struck midnight. Without a word to the Prince, Cinderella tore herself from his embrace, dashed down the grand staircase, and fled the palace. In her haste, she dropped one of her glass slippers.

The Prince was completely bewildered. 'Dearest, wait!' he called, running after her. 'I love you. I must see you again.'

But Cinderella disappeared from sight. She raced all the way home, where she fell into a deep sleep in front of the fire.

True to the Fairy Godmother's word, Cinderella was changed back to a simple maid dressed in ragged clothes. Dozing on the hearth, she dreamed of the ball.

When she shook herself awake, she was not sure what had happened. 'Was I really at the ball?' she asked herself, 'or was it all a wonderful dream?'

As she tried to decide, she reached into the pocket of her apron and, to her amazement, found a glass slipper. 'It *was* real,' she announced to herself. 'I *did* go to the ball and I *did* dance with the Prince.'

Suddenly, she heard her stepsisters returning from the ball. Cinderella quickly tucked the slipper into her apron pocket.

'The Prince found me irresistible,' purred Krvlyaka, hobbling around the room in her tight, uncomfortable shoes.

'That's what you think,' responded Zlyuka heatedly. 'He was far more interested in me.' As usual, the sisters continued bickering until there came a knock at the door. It was the Prince's page.

'The Prince fell in love with a lovely girl he met at the ball,' the page announced, 'but the girl fled before the ball was over. She dropped her glass slipper on the way out. The Prince is searching for the owner of the slipper, for he wishes to make her his wife.'

As Cinderella and the two stepsisters bowed deeply, the Prince entered their house. He held the glass slipper in his hand.

The older stepsister rushed forward to greet him. 'I'm sure the slipper will fit me,' she said. But, push as hard as she could, she was

unable to get her big foot into the tiny slipper.

Seeing her sister's failure, the younger stepsister approached the Prince. 'I knew it wouldn't fit her. It looks more like my size.' And she squeezed to get her foot in. So hard did she squirm and wriggle that she fell backward off her chair!

Cinderella ran over to help her stepsister. But when she bent over, the glass shoe fell out of her apron pocket.

'Why, it's the missing slipper!' cried out the Prince. 'You must be the girl I danced with at the ball. Come, try on this slipper.'

Cinderella appeared confused and shyly turned away.

'But she wasn't even *at* the ball,' Krivlyaka argued.

'She was here all night on the hearth,' insisted Zlyuka.

The Prince ignored the idle chatter of the two stepsisters. Kneeling before Cinderella, he gently guided her trim little foot into the slipper.

It fitted perfectly!

'So, you are the mysterious girl from the ball,' the Prince said in great excitement. 'How lucky I am to find you. You shall be my bride.'

At that moment Cinderella's Fairy Godmother appeared in the room. She raised her wand and blessed the lovely couple.

With another wave of her wand, the Fairy Godmother caused the old house to disappear. In its place, there sprang up a fragrant and enchanted garden filled with sparkling fountains and brightly coloured beds of roses and lilies and daisies. Inhabiting this gorgeous setting was a band of fairies who joined Cinderella and the Prince in celebrating their reunion.

As Cinderella and the Prince dreamily waltzed in each other's arms, a magical boat gently glided down beside them. Hand in hand, the lovers climbed aboard. And, with the fairies gaily waving good-bye, the couple sailed off to live happily ever after.

Firebird

Prince Ivan, heir to the throne of Russia, roamed through the dark, thick forest. In his hand, he held a tightly drawn bow. He was hunting and was ready to strike any creature that happened to be hiding in the thicket.

While crossing a clearing in the forest, Ivan heard a low cry from the surrounding trees. 'What's that?' he asked out loud, jumping back from the shadows.

There was no answer.

Suddenly, from above his head, a gold light appeared. Its brilliance lit up the whole open glade.

'Who's there?' called the Prince, trying to find the source of the light.

Silence. Search as he did, he could see nothing.

The light raced around and around the good Prince Ivan, almost blinding him. He ran off beneath the trees to hide in safety. From here, he watched a most wondrous scene.

A magnificent being, half-bird, half-woman, swooped into the forest clearing. She was the dazzling Firebird, the legendary magical bird of old Russia. Her face and arms were those of a charming young girl. The rest of her body was covered with brilliant red and yellow flamelike feathers. A long red feather extended from the top of her head.

Unaware of the hunter, the Firebird swooped about with wild abandon. She soared and glided, twirled and whirled, in complete freedom. Sometimes she came so close to Ivan that he could have reached out and touched her. Other times she hovered high above his head.

When the Firebird alighted for an instant, Ivan sprang forward and grasped the Firebird around her waist. She froze at his very touch. Her fluttering movements stopped and she became stiff with fear.

Slowly she started to struggle. Flinging back her beautiful head, she waved her arms and beat the air in a frenzied attempt to break away from her captor. But Ivan held her tightly in his arms.

'I beg you, let me go,' the frightened Firebird pleaded. 'I will die if I am not free.'

Touched by her beauty and sincerity, Ivan loosened his grip. The grateful Firebird dropped to one knee in a deep bow. She thanked the kind Prince for his pity and compassion. And to express her gratitude, the Firebird took from her breast a bright red feather.

'This feather is a magic charm,' she confided. 'Keep it with you always. If ever you are in trouble, no matter where, I will come to your aid.'

Ivan marvelled, 'You are truly a most remarkable creature. I thank you for this kind gift.'

Then, as the Prince watched, the Firebird flew off, quickly rising high in the sky.

Soon after the Firebird disappeared, twelve young, laughing princesses came running into the forest clearing. They were dressed in long peasant frocks with little caps.

The princesses danced happily together until someone noticed Prince Ivan watching them. Startled at the sight of a stranger in their midst, the girls huddled and whispered excitedly.

Ivan drew closer. 'Greetings, my lovely maidens,' he said, bowing in a respectful and half-serious way. 'Pray tell me who you are.'

The princesses were frightened by this request and cast anxious looks at the intruder. But Ivan insisted on an answer. He beckoned the prettiest girl, who seemed to be the leader, to come to him. She left the group and stepped forward to speak with the Prince.

'We are twelve princesses from different foreign lands,' the lovely girl explained. 'We were captured by the evil magician Kastchei, ruler of this monstrous forest kingdom. Anyone he catches on his lands, Kastchei turns into stone. For some reason, he didn't put us under that spell. Instead, he is holding us as prisoners forever. Our only joy is to dance.'

'Will you honour me with a dance?' the handsome Prince asked the young girl.

She nodded politely, and the two joined hands. The couple then led the entire group in a lively, Russian folk dance. Although the Prince and his chosen Princess tried to cling tightly to each other, the other girls playfully came between them and attempted to break their embrace. Even so, the two began to fall deeply in love.

'I want to help you,' Ivan told her. 'Come away with me, and we will be married.'

'No, no,' the Princess replied in great agitation. 'I cannot leave. And, if the wicked Kastchei finds you here, he will transform you into a stone statue. No, you must flee and save yourself.'

'My love for you is too strong,' Ivan insisted. 'I will happily make any sacrifice to have you as my own.'

'And I love you, Ivan,' said the Princess earnestly. 'But our love is doomed. I am under the sorcerer's evil spell.'

A trumpet suddenly sounded in the distance. The frightened girls shuddered, and a look of terror crossed the Princess's face. 'I must go now. Please, dearest, save yourself. Escape now from this cursed place.'

The Princess ran toward the castle of the cruel Kastchei. On her way, she looked back and called one last warning to Ivan, 'Don't try to follow me, or something terrible will surely happen.' With that, she disappeared.

Left alone, Ivan grew alarmed. The woods were now dark and menacing and he feared for his safety. But before he could escape, dozens of hideous monsters swarmed out of the threatening gloom. With a terrifying leap, they bounded towards him. Scaly and horned, the beasts were multicoloured – green, brown, blue, orange; one was more ugly and grotesque than the others. Some looked partly human but had the heads of bears, wolves, and alligators. Others were two-headed creatures never before seen on earth, with fanglike teeth extending over their lips. The monsters leapt and pranced around, beating and scratching at Ivan with their teeth and nails.

Ivan fought off the fiends with his sword as best he could. But the great numbers of jumping, crawling, rolling monsters threatened to overwhelm him.

Suddenly, the beasts stopped their attack. They fell back and bowed down as their master, Kastchei, entered, surrounded by the princesses.

'What are you up to, you disgusting vermin?' Kastchei growled at the monsters. The beasts fell all over each other, dodging Kastchei's withering stare.

Kastchei noticed Ivan. Pointing a finger with a long, talonlike fingernail at the Prince, he stormed, '*You*, what are *you* doing here?

Don't you know that anyone who enters my magical kingdom is turned to stone?'

The princesses circled around their cruel lord and implored him to forgive Ivan. But Kastchei fumed, 'Never! He must become another stone statue in my garden.'

So saying, Kastchei raised both hands over his head and recited the magical words, 'Ebra, Lebra, Membra, Mo.'

Ivan felt his body begin to grow stiff. Desperate to save his life, he suddenly recalled the Firebird's magic feather. Moving as fast as he could, he whipped out the bright red charm and waved it in the air.

In a flash, he heard a beating of wings and saw the Firebird glide down. Rushing to Ivan's side, she handed him the gleaming golden sword that she had been carrying. Ivan lunged at Kastchei with the sword. But the wicked magician was too fast for Ivan and scampered away unhurt. Again Ivan thrust at the evil man, who sidestepped the blow. Finally, Kastchei turned and fled into the dark shadows of the forest.

'Kastchei's soul is to be found in a giant egg hidden somewhere in this garden,' the Firebird instructed Ivan. 'Find that egg and smash it. Kastchei's wickedness will be destroyed forever.'

Ivan searched the entire garden. He chased back and forth, looking in the grass, around the bushes, behind the trees. He hunted hard and long, but he could not find it.

Just as he was about to give up, he spied a huge white egg tucked into the hollow trunk of an old tree. Ivan seized the egg and held it high over his head. With a mighty swing, he flung it down to the ground. The egg smashed and its contents poured out.

'The days of Kastchei are now over,' the Firebird exultantly proclaimed. 'His spells are broken. You can marry your Princess, Ivan.'

The Princess and Ivan joined hands. 'We will always be in your debt,' he said to the Firebird. 'You saved our lives and brought us great happiness.'

'You are a good man, Prince Ivan,' she answered. 'I wish you and

tea and munched biscuits to keep warm. Others just milled around, looking at the sights and chatting with their friends.

Peasants, soldiers, gypsies, landowners, and shopkeepers fell into step with the small band of musicians who mingled with the crowd. Servants, nannies, cooks, grooms, gardeners, and coachmen, all wearing their best uniforms, circled about talking noisily. The children chased one another in and out of the bustling crowd. And lovers walked hand in hand, kissing when no one was looking.

The entire city's population, it seemed, had turned out in holiday clothes to feast and celebrate before the start of the holy season. The sounds of their laughter and music echoed loudly in the cold, crisp afternoon.

Into this milling crowd pushed an organ grinder with a young girl dancer carrying a small rug and a triangle. She spread the rug on the snow and, striking the triangle with a steady beat, began to dance to the cheerful strains of the organ grinder's gay Russian folk song.

After a while, another organist and dancer took their places on the other side of the square. A small group gathered around the new dancer. Soon a contest began between the two performers as each tried to outdo the other. The first dancer twirled around, faster and faster. Then the other did the same dance, faster yet.

The fascinated spectators looked back and forth dizzily from one dancer to the other. Finally, the two dancers were exhausted and the competition was over. The audience applauded loudly and tossed coins at their feet, as the girls delightedly scooped up their reward.

Two drummers now stepped out of a large booth boldly decorated with a bright blue curtain across the front. Above it was a sign, written in Russian, with the words 'Living Theatre.' The drummers attracted the attention of the fairgoers, who looked on curiously as the musicians started a long loud roll on their instruments.

A man with a tall pointed hat and a black cloak covered with magic symbols, stuck his head out of the curtain. It was Charlatan, the magician, the owner of the Living Theatre.

From a deep pocket within his robe, Charlatan drew out a flute and started to play. The melody was sweet and gentle, rising and falling. It seemed a magical song, designed to call up some special mysterious powers.

As Charlatan played on, people in the crowd started to sway to the music's hypnotic beat. Over and over he repeated the tune, until suddenly he stopped and snapped his fingers at the booth. The curtains popped open, revealing three life-size puppets. Each one hung motionless, suspended from a big armrest.

In the middle was the Ballerina, with a perfect china-doll face, big round eyes, and bright red cheeks. Dressed in a light, frilly ballet tutu, she was posed in mid-step, as though waiting to continue her dance.

On the left was the Moor, his big, powerful body magnificently attired in a gold and black uniform. White circles around his eyes and mouth stood out in sharp contrast to his coal-black face. Just like the Ballerina, he looked as though he was about to jump off his perch.

On her other side was the clownlike Petrouchka, his clothes loosely hung over his limp and lifeless form. With his head lolling to one side, he looked like a rumpled rag doll, the least likely of the three to move or be moved.

The disagreeable-looking Charlatan then sounded his flute three more times. The puppets sprang instantly to life. Although they still hung from the armrests, their feet began tapping out a lively Russian dance. But after a few minutes, the Moor, the Ballerina, and Petrouchka jumped down from the armrests and into the square to continue their dance.

The crowd stepped back to give them room. The puppets started to act out a story of their own. Both the Moor and Petrouchka were in love with the Ballerina. But she preferred the Moor. This made Petrouchka very angry. He attacked the much stronger Moor. The Moor gave his rival a terrible thrashing.

As the three puppets presented the play, it was clear that they were not just acting. It was as though they were not puppets at all, but real, live people. And the story they were telling was not make-believe but a real happening. They were deadly serious.

The crowd grew increasingly apprehensive and fearful. Some people even panicked and began to shrink away.

Charlatan moved quickly to try to save the situation. He waved his hands in the air. The three puppets froze in place and quickly retreated to their armrests in the booth.

'It's nothing, folks,' Charlatan explained to the audience. 'They're just puppets acting out a story. It's all make-believe.' And he pulled across the blue curtain and disappeared inside the booth.

Behind the drawn drape, Charlatan seized the unhappy Petrouchka by his collar and flung him into his dark, cell-like room.

'This will teach you to go making trouble!' Charlatan roared as he left, locking the door behind him.

Petrouchka lay crumpled on the floor, weeping as though his heart would break.

Quite slowly, the puppet arose, with his knees turned in and his arms crisscrossed awkwardly across his limp torso. 'Nobody cares if I live or die,' he complained. 'The whole world is against me. I love the Ballerina, but she loves the Moor. Charlatan controls everything I say or do. And the Moor would like to kill me – and probably will!'

The more he thought about his situation, the more hostile and resentful Petrouchka became. The embittered clown stormed around his room. Just then, the Ballerina opened the door and came in.

'I was feeling sorry for you,' she explained, flashing Petrouchka a warm, friendly smile. 'How about a little visit?'

Petrouchka's spirits lifted at once. Delirious with joy and blissfully happy, he repeated over and over again, 'I love you, I love you, I love you.'

The Ballerina's smile faded. She recoiled from the urgency and intensity of his advances. 'Don't carry on so,' she scolded Petrouchka, with a look of disgust on her face.

In despair, Petrouchka cried even louder, 'But I love you. I love